Mrs Headon
"You said it!"

The Life & Endeavours
of Hefina Headon
with Memoirs
told by
Family & Friends

Jayne D Headon

MRS HELLFIRE, "YOU SAID IT!"

Copyright © 2015 Jayne D Headon.
All rights reserved.

First paperback edition printed 2015 in the United Kingdom A catalogue record for this book is available from the British Library.

ISBN 978-0-9933475-0-4

No part of this book shall be reproduced or transmitted in any form or by any means, electronic or mechanical, including photocopying, recording, or by any information retrieval system without written permission of the publisher. The memories and recollections within this book may not be historically or factually accurate therefore should not be used as a source of reference or as any fact finding medium.

Published by Headon Publishing
www.headonpublishing.co.uk

Edited by Emily Francis

Designed and Set by Headon Publishing

Fonts license by Jake Luedecke

Printed and Bound in Great Britain by Caktus, Christchurch, Dorset. 01202 484666
Cover Photography courtesy of Stuart and Christine Powell 1984

For more copies of this book, please email: Jayne@HeadonPublishing.co.uk
Tel: 07725577458

Although every precaution has been taken in the preparation of this book, the publisher and author assume no responsibility for errors or omissions. Neither is any liability assumed for damages resulting from the use of this information contained herein.

DEDICATION

To all who have once been, to all in the present and to all who are yet to come.
With love for you Mam, an inspiration to us all.
Always.

Contents page

Preface	VII
Prologue	VIII
Family Trees	XII

Section 1 - The Biography 1930 - 2013 — 1

Chapter 1 - The Early Years	3
Chapter 2 - Journey into Adulthood	10
Chapter 3 - The Challenging Era	13
Chapter 4 - Moving Forward	18
Chapter 5 - Community Spirit	24
Chapter 6 - Significant Differences (The Strike)	30
Chapter 7 - Rolling Along	49
Chapter 8 - A Grand Finale	58
Chapter 9 - Hefina's Legacy	67

Section 2 - Life in Photographs — 71

Chapter 1 - The Early Years	72
Chapter 2 - Journey into Adulthood	78
Chapter 3 - The Challenging Era	83
Chapter 4 - Moving Forward	94
Chapter 5 - Community Spirit	101
Chapter 6 - Significant Differences (The Strike)	108
Chapter 7 - Rolling Along	119
Chapter 8 - A Grand Finale	130
Chapter 9 - Hefina's Legacy	139

Section 3 - The Memoirs — 145

Family	147
Friends	216

Acknowledgements	269
A guide to Welsh pronounciation	271
Reference & Bibliography	274

PREFACE

My name is Jayne. I am the legal daughter of Hefina Headon. You will come to learn exactly who I am as you read through this biography. This book has been written as a legacy to Hefina. She has been an inspiration to me with all the good work she has done throughout her life. I am inspired by her determination and commitment to voluntary work in the community and wanted to leave behind a record of her life story for future generations to read and learn.

This biography contains photographs from family collections accumulated over the years and followed by a collection of memoirs from family and friends.

Whilst writing, I learnt that I may have started this book a little late, as there weren't so many people left to speak to who could have given me more of the information and stories that I searched for. I have also learned how time can fade memories and how difficult it has been for us to remember. Photographs have helped to identify some, but not others. The lack of writing on the back of these images made it difficult to piece time and place together.

I now feel far more inspired by my mother, I have grown in pride for such a stalwart and all that she has accomplished. I have travelled many miles to visit those who have offered their stories, and gained new knowledge and skills along the way.

My siblings, Ian and Alison have helped a great deal with the ground work of piecing together the timeline of Hefina's life and locating people with contact details and addresses. I have recorded the recollection of peoples experiences, and views of the person Hefina was. You will find these in Section three with acknowledgements located at the back of the book.

PROLOGUE

I give thanks to Pathé for allowing the use of passages taken from the press notes for the film Pride to inform this prologue.

2012

Stephen Beresford, a screenplay writer and David Livingstone, a producer from Calamity Films agreed to commission a script entitled 'Pride'.

Livingstone: "He (Stephen Beresford) told me this incredible story about a group of gay and lesbian activists and their relationship with striking miners in Wales. I was completely electrified. When you find a real story, you get a chemical reaction inside and when that happens you know you have something special. In that moment we set sail on the project."

Beresford: "David got it straight away as did Cameron McCracken, Pathé Productions' Managing Director, and they ran with it."

McCracken: "It is remarkable that this film even exists. A mainstream dramatic comedy about gay rights and trade unionism? A preposterous idea. Yet the film stands as proof that a brilliant screenplay in the hands of passionate filmmakers can squash all rational doubt."

Based on true events, Pride is a film about two worlds colliding and then entwining, a rousing celebration of the alliance between two disparate groups of people who came together over their shared history of oppression, shattering prejudices and forging unlikely friendships along the way.

Theatre Director Matthew Warchus was the perfect director for the material.

Warchus: "This was a script I just couldn't say no to, it made me laugh out loud, it surprised and delighted me at every turn, and it ultimately moved me to tears. It's a truly affirming and inspiring story, funny, honest and moving, and by the end of it you want to punch the air and cheer!"

Monday 7th October 2013

Narrow tables and lovely old wooden chairs were laid out in a banquette style with a big bar to the side. A Miners' lodge banner had been appliquéd and sewn together and donned the stage of the Onllwyn Miners' Welfare Club, the interior of which had been recreated in a school hall just outside London.

Red leather seating matched the red leather clad bar and orange 70's style curtains hung floor length on each window. Tables were set up for food parcel distribution. The atmosphere was taken from the real Onllwyn Miners' Welfare Hall situated in a very small village in the heart of the Dulais Valley in South Wales.

Film crew and actors were gathered, dressing rooms created and outfits sourced and fitted. It was the first day of filming 'Pride'.
News had arrived on set that Hefina Headon, Miners' committee secretary and stalwart, had passed away.

It was decided that as a mark of respect for Hefina, and fitting to her character, that a minute's applause would be appropriate (a minute's silence was not within her nature!) One of Britain's best character actresses, Imelda Staunton, who was to play Hefina's character, led the applause.

The filming began.

2 days earlier...

Saturday 5th October 2013, 2:45pm

The sun shone through the set of small French doors which opened out onto a concrete courtyard. Long heavy green curtains hung to each side of the doors. The room was painted green with cream hues accented by the curtains. A wooden bedside table was positioned by the metal hospital style bed. In the corner of the room stood a small table with two chairs on either side. Hefina lay half sat up in the bed; she had been suffering for a few days with pneumonia but felt slightly better this afternoon. It was time for her to try and eat; she asked for a pudding.

At 3pm the pudding arrived, but during the time it took the staff to return, Hefina had left this world, aged 83. Suffering with dementia for a few years and unaware of her surroundings, it was now time for her to leave this land behind and join those who waited for her, where peace would encompass her.

Good night and God bless.

X

FAMILY TREE
(Bold Deceased)
// Divorce symbol

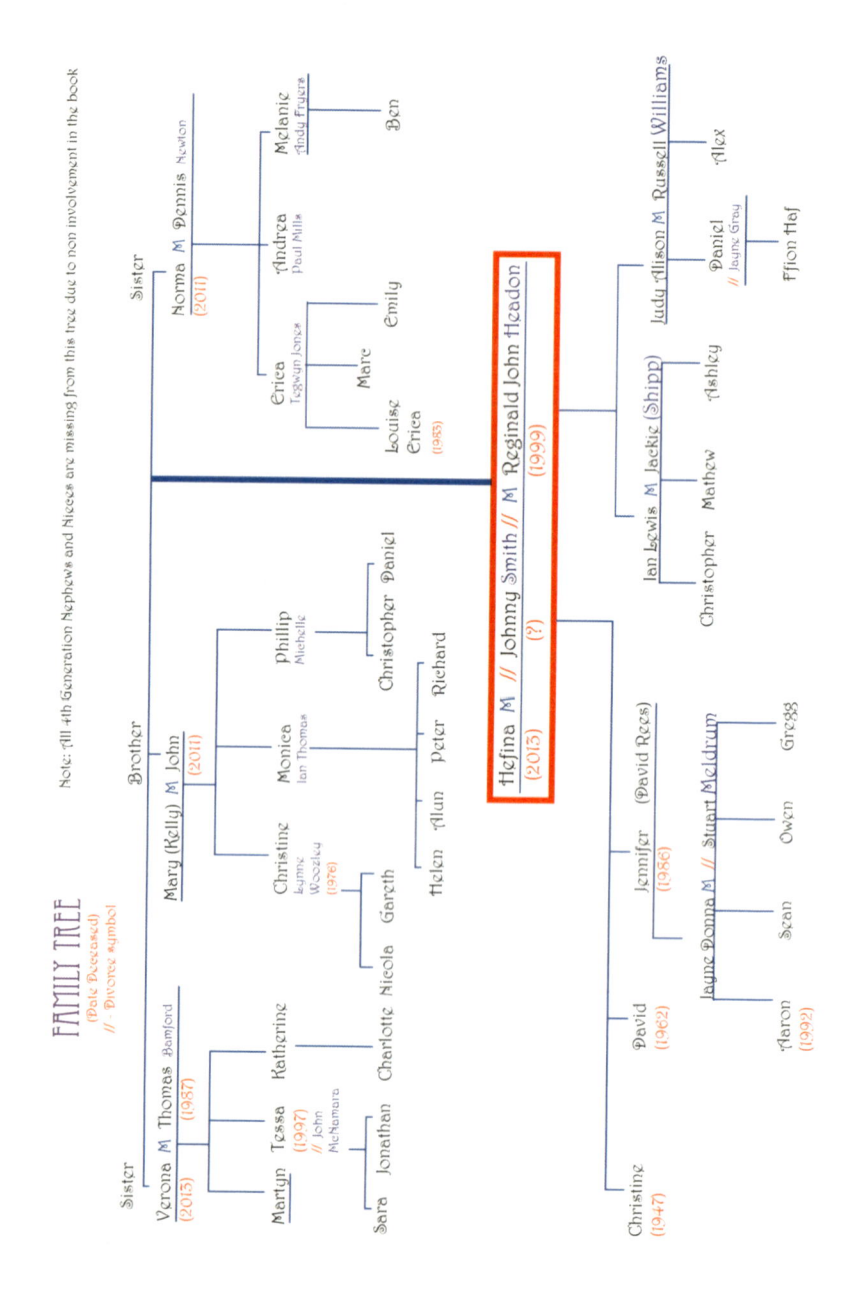

Note: All 4th Generation Nephews and Nieces are missing from this tree due to non involvement in the book

Sister — Brother — Sister

Verona M Thomas Bamford (1987)

Mary (Kelly) M John (2011)

Norma M Dennis Newton (2011)

Judy Allison M Russell Williams

Martyn   Tessa (1997) // John McNamara   Katherine

Christine Kumar Wozzku (1976)   Monica Ian Thomas   Phillip Michelle

Erica Tegwyn Jones   Andrea Paul Mills   Melanie Andy Fraser   Ben

Ian Lewis M Jackie (Shipp)   Daniel // Jayne Gray   Alex

Sara   Jonathan   Charlotte   Nicola   Gareth   Helen   Alun   Peter   Richard   Mare   Emily   Christopher   Mathew   Ashley   Ffion   Hef

Christopher   Daniel   Louise Erica (1985)

Hefina M // Johnny Smith // M Reginald John Headon
(2015)   (?)   (1999)

Christine (1947)

David (1962)

Jayne Donna M // Stuart Meldrum   Jennifer (David Rees) (1986)

Aaron (1992)   Sean   Owen   Gregg

XII

FAMILY TREE
EXTENDED FAMILY
(Date Deceased)
M = Divorce symbol

Louisa M John Philips (1954) (1954)

Martha M Joseph Lewis (1954)

- William (1918)
- Eva (1952) Will Davies (1986)
- Thomas (1980) Mara Lydia (1999)
- Richard (1972) Peggy (1999)
- Victor (1915)
- Bryn (1963) Louise (1999)
- Ronald (1922)

Catherine Louisa M Thomas Idris Lewis (1996) (1972)

Hefina (2013)

- May (1961)
- Oswald (1939)
- Vera (1908)
  - Audrey
  - Beryl (2009)
  - James
- Margaret (1977) William Hackes (1955)
  - Ann

- Lillian (1995)
- Iris (1977) John Bergen (1997)
- Terri Edith
- Nicholas
- Neil
- Glenn
- Bethan
- William (1977) Margaret
  - Mark
  - Richard

James M Rachel Hannah Smith (1961) (1986)

1st Husband David John Smith

Daniel M Hilda Mary Headon (1960) (1966)

- Joan (2001) Paddy Allen (1995)
  - Peter
- Lillian (2002) Pat Cook (2013)
  - James Gerald Larracombe
  - Christine
- Derek (1998)

2nd Husband Reginald John Headon (1999)

Note: Some Cousins, Nephews and Nieces are missing from this tree due to non involvement or mention in the book

XIII

Section 1

The Life & Endeavours

1930-2013

CHAPTER 1

The Early Years

"Situated between 'March-Howell', 'Hir-Fynnydd' and 'The Drum' Mountains, in an undisturbed beautiful landscape filled with green pastures and forests lies the Dulais Valley. Although left unspoilt for many centuries, The Dulais Valley did not escape the industrial revolution. The black diamond that lay beneath the soil did not go unnoticed, and during 1865, the railway was built that joined the valley with the town of Neath. This led to the sinking of the Seven Sisters Pits. Within years the men and their families who came to work at the collieries eventually renamed the village of Blaendulais the same as the Pit, and so the village of Seven Sisters was born."

Lewis, T.I. 1966

On a warm summer's morning of the 8th June, 1930 at a place called Brynhenllan, in an apartment owned by Mr and Mrs Jenkins, Hefina was born. She was the third child to Thomas and Katie Lewis. Hefina had two sisters and one brother: Verona born in January 1924, John born in July 1927 and Norma born in November 1935.

Hefina's name was created from the Welsh word for June 'Mehefin' Her father took away the 'M' and 'e' from the beginning of the word and added an 'a' on the end to give her the name Hefina – truly unique, as she turned out to be.

It was known to be a difficult time living at Brynhenllan. Mr and Mrs Jenkins were an unkindly pair. When the children were hungry, they found themselves sneaking food from their own pantry downstairs. Verona and John slept in the back bedroom above the living room, whilst Hefina slept with her parents in the front bedroom.

***

When Hefina was two and a half years old she woke from her sleep and alerted her mother with cries of "Mŵg! Mŵg!" (Smoke! Smoke!). Katie discovered that the living room was on fire and told Verona she had to stay on the landing and look after John and Hefina.

Verona remembers her mother, 27 years of age, in a white nightdress with no shoes having to go outside in waist high snow to get buckets of water to put out the fire on her own. Their father was at work and did not know about it until he came home. All the underclothes and Tommy's working clothes had been burned, as an 8 year old Verona remembers having to wear her grandmother's clothes and button boots to go to school.

It was an heroic act for a small child who saved her family from the fire through shouting her warnings. It would seem that Hefina was quite vocal from a very young age.

***

It was 1933 when Thomas Idris Lewis bought a ready to erect asbestos building and built his new bungalow on purchased land in Dulais Road. They named it Tan-y-Coed and this was to be Hefina's home for the rest of her childhood.

The bungalow was surrounded by fields. Tommy worked tirelessly digging the gardens, he planted lawns and small topiary hedgerows at the front, with formal pathways of rose bushes and seasonal flowers. The back garden comprised of his vegetable patches, where he grew peas, potatoes, beans and other seasonal fare. There were steep steps which led up to street level. From the top of the steps the bungalow looked beautiful and quaint in its tranquil setting with the rise of 'Mynydd Y Drum' as its backdrop.

***

The village infants school opened on the 14th December, 1908. In 1927 Miss E Rees was appointed to take charge. By the time Hefina attended in 1935, Miss Rees' sister was also teaching at the school, they were known as Miss Rees Fawr (large) and Miss Rees Fach (small). The sisters lived in a large house at the end of Pen-y-Banc, tucked away in the corner alongside the gate to the 'cwm' (grass valley) where the railway ran adjacent to the street. John Headon (who she would later marry) was also in her class.

* * *

During Hefina's first year at school, at the age of 5, whilst standing in front of the open fire to warm before bed time, the back of her nightdress caught fire. The garment melted rapidly onto her skin as she screamed in fear and pain. Her father swaddled her in wet towels and blankets and rushed her to the nearest hospital. Her burns were severe but she was lucky the flames didn't reach her neck and face. The nurses had to peel her nightdress from her to reveal the extent of the burns. Throughout the duration of this horrific incident her parents were kept away for fear of infection. It was an anxious time for a young child in trauma. Her six week stay in hospital was longer than she could endure and she wept for her mother. When the time came, she was overjoyed to be going home. Although scarred, she recovered well from her ordeal.

* * *

World War II began when Hefina was 9 years old. In the first year of the war, 15 miles away from Seven Sisters, Swansea Docks were being targeted by the German Luftwaffe. The blackouts were enforced and the villagers watched the skies light up as the bombs dropped, leaving faint blasts in the distance.

"*The first air raid on Swansea was heralded by a golden flare which lit the sky ablaze at 3:30am on June 27, 1940. Guided by this glow, the Luftwaffe easily found their target and dropped 10 High Explosives over the east side of Swansea. The residential area of Danygraig was rudely awakened to the realities of war as the bombs dropped amongst its streets. Although the raid caused some damage to properties, there were amazingly no casualties. Together with the fact that 4 of the bombs which had fallen upon Kilvey Hill failed to explode, this initial attack was relatively ineffectual, but it did succeed by striking real fear, shock and trepidation into the hearts of Swansea's civilians.*

What followed for Swansea during the years of World War II was to test the very spirit of the people who struggled to continue life against the backdrop of conflict, bombs, terror, destruction and death. The lowest point came in February, 1941 during what is commonly referred as 'The Three Nights' Blitz'. It lasted for nearly 14 hours, killed 230 people, injured another 397, wiped out entire streets of residential houses, made 7,000 people homeless and left the town centre a terrifying inferno of total destruction."

Explore-Gower online

Back in the Dulais Valley, the families could see the skies light up from the bombs and the flares. Fire and black billowing smoke filled the air in the distance. It was a frightening time of an unknown future.

One dark evening the winds were exceptionally high. During the black outs, lights were not to be taken down to the toilet at the bottom of the garden, so with her little gas mask in a cardboard box around her neck, Hefina braved the storm and headed for the 'ty bach' (toilet). The building was a shack situated at the bottom of the garden backing onto the rear fence which led into the fields behind. As Hefina sat blissfully unaware, a gust of wind travelled through the building, lifting it off its blocks and hurling it into the fields behind, with Hefina still sat on the toilet clinging for dear life. Luckily this time she was not harmed and managed to climb out of the mangled outhouse and back into the bungalow safely where she told her family of her ordeal.

* * *

All the children in the family were expected to attend Sunday School at Soar Congregational Chapel, Pen-y-Banc, Blaendulais. This was known as Eglwys Annibynnol Soar (an independent Christian faith)where her father, Tommy, became a deacon. He kept 'Mintoes' in his pockets to keep the children quiet during the service, which he handed out surrepticiously with a wink as they filed past.

* * *

Hefina's grandparents on her father's side, Joseph Lewis and his wife Martha, came to live in Seven Sisters for the work that was available. Martha Richards came down from Merthyr originally to live in Ystalyfera. A lot of people moved there to work at the tin works. There was a brickworks in Brynteg which Martha worked at, she would walk across the mountain to go to work each day. She was a very strong woman.

Joseph worked and lived in Ystalyfera, which is where they met and married. They moved from there to Price's Row in Coelbren because he got a job in the colliery in Onllwyn. Tommy and his sister, Maggie were born in Price's Row. Later they were given a house in Mary Street, Seven Sisters which Martha thought was wonderful. One day Martha told Joseph that she was not going to move again, she told him to go on his own; he wanted to move collieries, and so he walked out. No one saw him again. He ended up living out his days in the workhouse in Ammanford!

* * *

Hefina's Grandmother on her mother's side, Louisa Phillips (known as Nana to the grandchildren) owned a milk round. All of the children had to help with the milk round when they could. Louisa lived at Breakon Villa, 40 Martyn's Avenue. Nana was a very strong and authoritative woman. Everyone did what Nana said without any question. When her husband John (known as Papa) was still alive they used to be part of the local amateur dramatics society. They would often don costumes and act at every opportunity. Nana was quite an inspiration to Hefina and this would have been where she acquired her love of dressing up.

Below is an extract taken from Mrs Valerie James' photo book of her memories. Val went to school with Hefina, she was a year younger than her. They were part of the same gang of children during their childhood.

"Mrs Phillips went up to the train station to collect milk from the Brecon train and she delivered to customers this milk from urns in a cart as there were no milk bottles at this time. I would take out a jug and she would measure the amount of milk I wanted with a pint or half pint ladle and pour it into the jug. The cart had just a strip of wood across the back end on the floor. When she finished her rounds she would hold the horses' reins with one hand and crack the whip with the other hand and race off down the road with the dust flying everywhere.

The miners' that were exempt from going to war would have to join the home defence such as home guards or join the fire brigade. As children, we found out there was going to be an exercise by the home guards where half would be the enemy and take the railway signal box and the other half would defend it. This was to take place on a Saturday afternoon. The railway line went on a viaduct bridge over the river towards the signal box. About ten or more of us children were making mud balls all week. We added small stones and dried them out in the sun before we hid them behind bushes and trees. When Saturday came we were all there hiding in secret places where we could not be seen. When the whistle blew for the start of the operation to take the signal box, both sides of the home guards did not know what was happening as they were being bombarded with mud balls from everywhere. We did not know who was on what side so everyone was being pelted with mud and stones. Will Davies, the acting captain, called halt to everything, and told us children to go home and stop fraternising with the enemy. Big Will Davies, as he was known, frightened the life out of us and we did not know what fraternising meant. By Monday morning, the men working at the collieries and members of their own home guards had banners reading 'Seven Sisters home guards were over run by children and lost manoeuvres!"

* * *

Aged 11, Hefina was to find herself back at the hospital. This time she had contracted Diptheria. In the 30s this was the third leading cause of death in children in England and Wales. The infection is caused by bacteria passed from person to person through infected respiratory droplets affecting the nasal passage, tonsils and larynx.

On arrival, the hospital stripped her of her clothes and burned them as a process of killing the airborne droplets. She had in her possession a favourite toy, but this too was sent to be burned. She was left with nothing. Hefina was put into isolation to prevent the spread of infection. She spent another three weeks in hospital. During this time she tried everything she could to be discharged. She even tried to fool the nurses by pretending to eat the food, she used to throw handfuls of tapioca pudding behind her high headboard railings into the window recess behind her! The nurses would find lumps stuck to the window frame and sills. She fretted terribly not being able to see any of her family, only her mother was allowed access to the ward to see her daughter but she wasn't permitted to stay for long. Hefina soon recovered with medication and was welcomed home once again.

* * *

Grammar school was next for Hefina, having achieved the 11 plus, she travelled to the town of Neath to attend the grammar school. She did well in her academic subjects and paid much attention to her school work.

Hefina would leave school at the age of 14. Tommy wanted his daughter to have a good education and believed that secretarial skills would be her forte. He proceeded to teach her Pitman Shorthand in which he was self taught. In the meantime they saved all they could and paid for Hefina to attend the Swansea Secretarial College of Further Education.

CHAPTER 2

Journey Into Adulthood

After Nana Phillips' death the milk round was taken over by Hefina's mother, sometimes known as 'Katie Phillips the milk'.

On her rounds, Katie delivered milk to the Thomas family home. Mr Thomas had bought the Seven Sisters Post Office for his daughter Betsie. Katie spoke with the family and asked if they would consider giving Hefina a trainee post mistress position, under the instruction of their daughter Mrs Betsie MacCutcheon. They agreed and she began her training.

On 1st August, 1944 Hefina and another young girl named Iris joined Betsie. They filled the Post Office with cards and sweets. The telephone exchange was also situated in the Post Office and so they were to learn how to use this too. Later she would move onto other work opportunities, but for now she had secured herself a career.

As a teenager Hefina grew fond of a boy named John Headon. They had been in school together since the age of 5. Aged 14, John began to work at the colliery. They were close friends but their companionship was frowned upon by Hefina's father. He discouraged her from seeing him as he felt John was a bad influence; John was a smoker and a bit of a 'chap'.

Despite her father's objections, Hefina continued to go out dancing and socialising with the village boys in the Dulais Valley. Norma (Hefina's younger sister) was sent out to accompany her as a chaperone and to tell their father what Hefina got up to! She met Johnny Smith, a 'Banwen boy' from a nearby village who had been adopted by James and Rachel Smith as a baby. He had come from Scotland to join his new family in Wales. They spent time together and enjoyed each others company, but things were about to change dramatically for Hefina. At the age of 16 she fell pregnant, and to the disgrace of her family, Hefina wanted to marry Johnny Smith.

Exactly one month after Hefina's 17th birthday, the wedding took place on the 8th July, 1947 at Soar Chapel. An announcement was posted in the local newspaper the following week. It read:

"The wedding was solomnised at Soar Chapel on Tuesday last week between Miss Hefina Lewis, daughter of Mr and Mrs TI Lewis, Tan-y-Coed, Seven Sisters, and Mr David John Smith son of Mr and Mrs James Charles Smith, 13 Heol-y-Marchog, Banwen. The Rev. Howell William officiated and the organist was Mrs M Price.

Given away by her father, the bride was attired in a gown of ivory chiffon velvet, with full length veil held in place by a wreath of orange blossoms. She carried a bouquet of saffron pink rosebuds. The matrons of honour, Mrs Verona Bamford and Mrs Iris Morgan wore gowns of pink and turquoise figured taffeta, respectively, with feathered headdresses, and carried bouquets of sweet peas. The bride was presented with a silver horseshoe by her cousin Kerry Dorgan. Mr William Williams was the best man and Mr John Lewis the groomsman. Over 40 guests attended the reception, which was held at the Waverley Hotel, Neath, where numerous telegrams were read. The groom's gift to the bride was a pearl necklace and the bride's gift to the groom was a signet ring, while the bridesmaids received pearl earrings surmounted with diamonds. The honeymoon was spent at Carmarthen. The bride travelled in an off-white coat with brown accessories. The bride was on the staff of the Seven Sisters Post Office, while the bridegroom has been an active member of the Onllwyn Y.M.C.A. for many years."

The couple moved into rented rooms at the Wynacott's home in Martyn's Avenue. Later that year their first child was born but tragically she was stillborn. They named her Christine and buried her in Tonna which is near the town of Neath.

Hefina fell pregnant again and in April, 1949 their second child David was born.

During Hefina's second pregnancy Johnny joined the Army. He completed his training with the Corps of Royal Electrical and Mechanical Engineers (REME) and was stationed in B Coy 1st FR

GBM in Blandford Forum, Dorset. At this time, things were not looking too good for the marriage, as Johnny omitted to pay Hefina any housekeeping money. She found herself having to apply to the county court of Glamorgan where Johnny was found guilty 'of wilful neglect to provide reasonable maintenance for her and her infant child'. David at the time was just 3 months old.

Hefina and David moved from Martyn's Avenue to number 13 Heol Marchog, Dyffryn Cellwen with James and Rachel Smith.

Just over a year later, Johnny was deployed to Tripoli, North Africa. His family was able to join him there and so Hefina and David left, travelling by boat to North Africa to be with him. However, they only remained there for 6 months. Up until this time the British had governed, but in 1951 they declared independence thus the bulk of the British forces began to leave.

On returning to Britain, Hefina and David returned to her childhood home at Tan-y-Coed. Johnny continued to serve his time with the Army.

In October, 1952 Hefina and Johnny were to have their third and final child, Jennifer. Hefina was suspicious by now that Johnny was having an affair. Her brother John was furious and threatened to 'get' Johnny. He was demanded to remain in the house by his father and not to cause trouble. Tommy Lewis wrote a letter to his solicitor, Mr T D Windsor Williams who instructed an investigator to follow Johnny Smith and record his findings. On 1st December, 1952 they heard back with information regarding this investigation.

On 19th December, 1952 she was back at the petty sessional division of Neath County Court serving a petition regarding legal custody of David aged 3 and a half and Jennifer aged 2 months. The court heard that 'on or about the 14th day of November, 1952 and on several subsequent occasions Johnny has been guilty of adultery'.

Glamorgan Constabulary's Police Woman Mary Garpanini served a divorce petition to Johnny Smith at 12 Gnoll Bank, Neath on 23rd December, 1952. By 30th June, 1953 Hefina was in receipt of the Decree Absolute and the marriage was officially dissolved.

CHAPTER 3

The Challenging Era

By 1953 Hefina was fully trained as a post mistress and so became relied upon for holiday cover throughout the Glamorgan area. She worked in numerous Post Offices up and down the valleys including Dyffryn Cellwen, Glyn Neath, Cwmgwrach, Resolven, Neath, Penrhiwtyn and Crynant. She became well known and liked by the Post Office sector and attended many nights out and conferences with them.

Destined to be together, her childhood friend John Headon became a prominent part of Hefina's life while she went through her divorce with Johnny Smith, who had been known to raise his hand to Hefina on occasions. This enraged and disgusted John Headon and made him more determined to protect and love her as he always had.

John was the youngest of three children born to Daniel and Hilda Mary Headon. John entered this world on 25th June, 1930 only a few weeks after Hefina. He had two older sisters, Lillian and Joan. The years between Joan and John were very few and the two became very close as brother and sister.

Hefina and John began to court. They spent many an evening out with friends at various dances held in the Onllwyn Miners' Welfare and RAFA clubs. When they danced, they seemed to be dancing on air, lighter than feathers. They were truly enjoyable to watch as they gaily glided around the dance floor. Dressed to suit the occasion, John always looked dapper in his suits, ties or bows and Hefina clad in her jewellery, with ritzy knee length dresses which flowed as John paraded her elegantly around the shiny dance floor. They often danced to live bands.

All of Hefina's siblings were married by this time and some had started their families too. Verona married Tommy Bamford and had Martyn, Tessa and later Katherine. John married Mary Kelly and had Christine, Monica and then Phillip. Norma married Dennis Newton and had Erica, Andrea and Melanie.

John's sisters were also married; Lillian to Dai Cook who had children Janice and Derek and Joan married Ronald (Paddy) Allan who had Peter.

On 22nd March, 1958 John and Hefina got married at Soar Chapel. Hefina wore a beautiful deep blue two piece velvet suit. Blue was her favourite colour. The bridesmaids were her own daughter Jennifer and her nieces Christine and Tessa. They wore pretty cream dresses with tan coloured coats and hats to match. John wore a brown suit, this was always his preferred colour of garment. Her nephews Martyn and Peter, along with her son David, also enjoyed the day.

Later that year they moved to 29 Heol Hen, Seven Sisters as new tenants on the estate. The house was a 1950's semi detached pebble dashed building and was situated just metres away from John's father and mother, Daniel and Hilda Headon. They owned a piece of land just behind 29 Heol Hen, it was number 6 Pen-y-Banc. Daniel had a large six car garage erected on the land, this left just over an acre of land for John's use.

Number 29 was unusual because pedestrians used the garden as a short cut path from the estate to the middle of Pen-y-Banc, an ideal walking route to the village centre. This didn't phase the Headons, friendly as they were, everyone was welcome, and felt comfortable to walk through, sometimes stopping on the way for a catch up on the local gossip and news.

During this time both David and Jennifer fluctuated between living in Heol Hen with their mother, and down at the Tan-y-Coed bungalow with their grandparents whilst Hefina and John worked. Neither David nor Jennifer was officially adopted by John Headon.

Although John Headon was a miner, he also ran a taxi service. He was a studious driver and joined his father's taxi service: Dan Headon's Taxis, telephone number - Seven Sisters 233!

John had acquired many horses (another of his passions) which he kept on the field opposite the house. He bought a few unused old railway carriages for the horses' stables and to house the feed and keep the tack dry.

On 7th April, 1960 John and Hefina welcomed the birth of their first child together. They named him Ian Lewis Headon.

The following few years were to bring physical and emotional turmoil to Hefina's life. Whilst nurturing Ian as a baby, David fell ill. He was weak at school and bullied by a teacher for his inability to be 'sporty'. The devastating news came in 1961 when David was diagnosed with Leukaemia. Sadly David's life was not destined to be a long one, from this moment onwards he rapidly deteriorated. Hefina gave up her work at the Post Office to care for him.

During the 1950s and early 60s, childhood Leukaemia was still untreatable in many areas. Some offered rudimentary and intensive chemotherapy, usually consisting of a single drug, but many children died soon after their diagnosis. It wasn't until the mid 60s through combining drugs, it meant that around five to ten percent of children diagnosed with this blood cancer were now being completely cured. Unfortunately this came too late for David and on 30th June, 1962 he passed away whilst his sister Jennifer sat reading stories to him from her favourite book. He was just 13 years old.

He was buried on 6th July, 1962 at Pen-y-Banc Cemetery.

Meanwhile, Hefina found herself pregnant with her fifth child. Finding it extremely difficult to cope with a 10 year old daughter, a small toddler and a dying son, being pregnant was not the joyous occasion that it should have been, but Hefina battled through. She gave birth to another daughter, Judy Alison, on 28th January, 1962.

* * *

Jennifer moved from her grandparents to live with her mother at the house in Heol Hen. One evening in 1963, whilst John and Hefina were at a concert dance in the Onllwyn Welfare, Jennifer had a terrible accident. She was 11 years old and had fallen over the handlebars of her bicycle. A man brought her home in his car. Nana Headon was babysitting the children at the time. Jennifer was unrecognisable; she had a bloodied face with glass embedded in her upper lip and cheeks. At this point, Hefina felt that hospitals were the most horrendous places, but off she went to be by her daughter's side. Jennifer recovered fully but suffered facial pain throughout her life from the resulting scars.

Hefina tried to put her life back together and returned to work. Her children attended school and Sunday School. Jennifer attended Cadoxton Comprehensive but Ian and Alison went to the Welsh speaking junior school in the village, Ysgol Gynradd Gymraeg Blaendulais.

As Hefina had come to expect, life wasn't a smooth ride for her. In 1967, at the age of 14 Jennifer fell pregnant. This was shunned upon but so much of it was going on. The done thing was to send your child away to be 'looked after' during the pregnancy in a discreet manner. Once Jennifer began to show signs of being pregnant, she was taken to the convent for a while and was later transferred to the Salvation Army home for unmarried mothers in Cardiff. On 16th January, 1968 Jayne Donna Smith was born under what was known as 'twilight sleep' (meaning Jennifer felt little pain and had no memory of the birth). After a short spell at the Barndardo's orphanage (paid for by the family), Jayne was brought home. She was officially adopted by John and Hefina in 1970 and was brought up as their daughter (and as Jennifer, Ian and Alison's sister) until she learned of her adoption at the age of 9.

Life was getting busy at 29 Heol Hen, John bought a mini bus to use as a family car and for the taxi service which he now named RJ Headon and Son. His first new taxi was a 1968 Ford Transit (registration MWN 87F). He owned two Austin vans before this. They also owned a caravan which had its own coal fire and chimney built in. They only went away in it once before it became stationary on the field for the children to play in and more horse related paraphernalia stored there until it started to fall apart.

Not only were there now four children to feed, John also cared for horses. He kept Silver, which was Ian's horse and Sian which was for Alison to ride. Later Sian had a foal who they named Suzie for Jayne. By 1972, sadly, John had given the horses to his friend, Benny, who lived on the farm at the bottom of the village. Benny kept his horses on the mountains, so John was able to call Sian whenever she was near. He missed her dearly; a few whistles on a windy day would have her galloping home to see him.

The family's involvement with the Pony Club started during these years (1960s), when Hefina became a member of the Banwen Pony Club committee.

The 'Miners' Fortnight' (a two week annual holiday) was spent with the Pony Club at Parc Le Breos Farm in the Gower. Their time was comprised of the men having competitions and women getting involved in games. The days were packed with riding horses on the beach, pony trekking and the farmer would hold a Gymkhana and invite the local pony clubs to join in for the day.

The adults enjoyed these holidays as much as the children. The older children were left in charge of the younger ones whilst the men and women spent the evenings in The Gower Inn. Occasionally some of the older children would also go into the pub and have a glass or two of cider.

In the 70s these holidays moved from the farm to Tenby, without the horses, just a convoy of caravans occupying a plot on the caravan park of their choice.

In addition to these wonderful holidays, Hefina also helped to organise a Christmas trip to the pantomime every year, but it had to be one of Stan Stennet's pantomimes held at either the Porthcawl Pavillion or the New Theatre in Cardiff. These trips were always great fun, with a long journey home. The bus often stopped for the men to use the toilets; they would not often come to the pantomime but spend the evening in a local pub! This would rile the women and the bus would be rife with cross women, drunken men and laughing children.

CHAPTER 4

Moving Forward

"On 9th January 1972 the British miners' went on strike for the first time since 1926. The strike lasted for seven weeks and 135 pits closed in South Wales. A state of emergency was declared and to economise on electricity Edward Heath's government had to reduce the working week to three days. As a result of the strike, the miners' wages were increased, becoming the highest among the British working class."

National Library of Wales

It was the summer of 1971 when the Onllwyn Post Office came up for sale. With encouragement from Betsie MacCutcheon, Hefina and John borrowed money from her father, Tommy, and bought the Post Office. They moved into their new home during August of that year.

Decimalisation had been introduced in February. The Post Office helped the children to familiarise themselves with this; Hefina had a small book that identified the new coinage which was always on hand.

Jennifer had left home by this point and lived in Swansea with her friends. While she was training to become a croupier in the local casinos she also worked at the Aluminium, Wire and Cable Company. Once she gained experience as a croupier she moved to London where she lived for many years working for Playboy and other large popular casinos.

Not long after the move, on 8th March, 1972 at around 4pm, Hefina's father Tommy Lewis passed away. It was an extremely sad time for the whole family, Tommy was the leading figure of the Lewis family and earned much respect from all who knew him. Katie, who was treasured and adored by Tommy, was distraught. She was not present at home the day he passed away, her sister Lil who lived with them was with him. This later became a grudge Katie could never let go of.

Following his passing, Katie became ill. After a long spell in hospital where she suffered with pernicious anemia, she was unable to stay at Tan-y-Coed. She needed specialist care that Lil was unable to give to her. Hefina took her mother into the Post Office for some time, and converted the parlour into a bedroom for her. Later, Lil also came to live with them, prior to this she stayed with Verona.

They remained with the family until a flat became available at the warden assisted home in the village. It was a newly built establishment in the heart of Seven Sisters, it was known as Canolfan, with easy access to the bus stop and the local 'VG' shop, chemist, ironmongers and chip shop. Katie and Lil lived there until their own passings many years later.

* * *

"By 4th February 1974 the miners' situation had deteriorated and a national miners' strike was called again. This strike lasted four weeks. A state of emergency and a three-day working week were once again declared."

National Library of Wales

Due to the shortage of energy emerging from the two strikes, power cuts were to become common place in the 70s. Hefina however, always had a good supply of candles and matches and plenty of drawing paper and games for the children to occupy themselves with.

During their time in Onllwyn, not long after the 1974 miners' strike, John sold his mini bus and bought a white Vauxhall Victor estate car (registration G872 YPA!) He was unable to repair the rusty old mini bus, it broke down regularly and was a financial drain. John held a contract at the time to transport the women workers to the factory in Rhigos. Idris and Davies Buses of Glynneath had 52 and 45 seater coaches and offered him a job as a driver. John did not own a badge for driving larger coaches and buses so was unable to take the position. Later Longs Buses of Abercrave offered him a part time position which he continued long into his retirement.

It was now time for Hefina's activist role to come into force when she campaigned for school transport to the Welsh School in Seven Sisters for the children of Banwen, Onllwyn and the first row of houses on Golwg-y-Bryn. Previously the children had been expected to travel to school on public transport, not the most suitable way to travel for the little children. Faraleigh Mini Buses won the contract to provide transport and John became the driver of the mini bus. It was around this time that Hefina became known to John as 'Hellfire' due to her formidable and stubborn personality.

Struggles were soon to appear once again for Hefina. In 1974 the remittance payments had just been delivered to the Post Office and were left on the counter. Jayne was ill upstairs in the house and calling for Hefina to see her. She left the Post Office unattended for no more than five minutes. On her return to the counter she saw that the money had been stolen. The owners of the Post Office had to pay any thefts from their own finances. This was very difficult, but the family helped Hefina and together they found enough to pay off the theft.

Hefina's niece, Erica came to train at the Post Office as a post mistress. She would work with Hefina during the week, this helped with ensuring that the shop was not left unattended and the potential to be burgled was reduced.

* * *

Not only was Hefina the village post mistress and a full time mother, she was also still involved with the Banwen Pony Club, whose field was positioned directly behind the Post Office. She was also heavily involved with the Pinafore Club at the Y.M.C.A in Dyffryn Cellwen.

The Banwen Pony Club was always a passion of John's. Hefina was always seen to be supportive (although there is no recollection of her ever wanting to mount a horse in her life!) On gymkhana days you could find her with the other wives and mothers in the pavillion making and serving food and refreshments.

In 1977, the club qualified for the final round of the Prince Philip Cup Games at the Horse of the Year Show in Wembley, London, where they brought home the trophy. It was a truly fantastic event and the atmosphere was euphoric when the riders made their lap of honour around the event ring. It was very emotional, a great day for all and was celebrated accordingly with plenty of alcohol and pride.

Hefina would sell raffle tickets or help raise funds for every event and good cause in the community. The Y.M.C.A held Easter Bonnet parades each year as well as concerts, pantomimes and plays, and held many activities and clubs using the premises (brownies, cubs and scouts). Discos were also held for the children; it was a place for youngsters to create their own music bands and hold concerts.

In 1975, Hefina's involvement with the Y.M.C.A saw her arrange the visit of Frankie Vaughan (an English singer of easy listening and pop music who became famous in 1940). Frankie was a member of the Lancashire Lads club, which was a major contributor to the National Association of Boys clubs in the UK and was welcomed by the boys of Banwen.

It would become apparent around these times that Hefina was partial to dressing up, and was always game. As part of the Pinafore Club she helped to organise the carnivals eash year. You could guarantee that she would be dressed up and parading the long procession from Roman Road in Banwen to the Field at Onllwyn on Carnival day.

John and Hefina never let life get in the way of their social calendar. They could always be found in a club or pub on a Friday and Saturday night, securing family members as babysitters for the children. As they grew up, the older children were expected to look after the younger ones, and they were never too far away if there was any trouble.

The Onllwyn Miners' Welfare Club was situated next door to the Post Office across the dirt track that led to the Pony Club and football fields. This had always been a place where they would attend concerts and events, but it wasn't the only place in Onllwyn. The Onllwyn Inn lay at the bottom of the village. It was a run down establishment until it was taken over by Malcolm and Anne Hathaway from Bargoed. Ian was to become familiar with the Onllwyn Inn and encouraged Hefina and John to support Malcolm and Anne. They visited and became very good and devoted friends. Their son Gordon was also to become good friends with Jayne and later they would play in the Dulais Valley Silver Band together.

On 15th February, 1977 Ian left for the Royal Navy. After seven weeks away for basic training Ian was allowed home for the weekend, as were the rest of his fellow sailors. However, his best friend, Paddy (Eric Samson), who came from Belfast was unable to go home. Ian mentioned this to his mother who immediately offered Paddy to come to Wales. He was treated as another member of the family and returned many times over the years.

During that particular weekend in April 1977, things were to change in regard to Hefina and John's involvement with the Onllwyn Welfare. Jennifer was home visiting for Easter and she had accompanied them there that evening. A fight broke out involving John and two other men. Ian helped to break up the fight.

The committee held a disciplinary meeting for John. The outcome found John to be banned from the club for a short while and after this, John decided not to go back to the club for many years. He would become a regular at the Onllwyn Inn where he then became part of the pool team.

Since moving to Onllwyn, Hefina began to feel unwell and she was diagnosed with an underactive thyroid. Her legs and neck became swollen with oedema and she then lost both her sense of taste and smell, which unfortunately never returned. She became lethargic and very tired, her muscles ached, she gained weight and experienced numbness and tingling in her fingers, but she still battled on.

The summer of 1977 brought Queen Elizabeth II's Silver Jubilee. Street parties were arranged up and down the country. Hefina was on the Jubilee Committee. The street party was held at the Onllwyn Welfare Hall and souvenirs were obtained for everyone, in particular commemorative coins and mugs. The party was flush with traditional 70's party food which included cheese, pineapple and pickles on cocktail sticks as well as cocktail sausages with mountains of sandwiches cut into triangles!

In 1978 a second burglary occurred. The family tried to cover it up by paying back the stolen money from Hefina's own wages over many months. Sadly the anomaly was still discovered and they had to leave the Post Office after the auditors came and discovered that the takings were down.

They were given a council house and left in the summer of 1978 after six years living in Onllwyn. It was to be the end of an era for Hefina, she would never earn an income or work again.

CHAPTER 5

Community Spirit

19 Cae Mawr, Seven Sisters was to be the family's new home. It was the summer of 1978 and although it rained quite a bit during this summer, the day of the move went well. The house was a pebble dashed three bed semi-detached, situated in a cul-de-sac on the council estate which was known locally as 'the site'.

Hefina's brother John also lived in the street with his family at number 9. On the day of the move their son Phillip helped, fetching and carrying and keeping Jayne company. John and Hefina had the master bedroom, Alison took the next one and Jayne was to sleep in the box room. This was the first time the girls had a room each.

From this time onwards Hefina had been advised not to work and was put on 'the sick' by the doctors. Not only was she suffering with Thyroid disorder and the onset of type 2 Diabetes, she was also still going through the menopause, but this didn't faze Hefina.

The cul-de-sac was a very friendly place, there were lots of children of all different ages and the women warmed to Hefina. She knew many people already and made new friends too. There was a young boy who lived in the cul-de-sac, named Michael, who was diagnosed with arthritis from a very young age. The women of the street decided to begin an Arthritis Fundraising Committee to raise money for the hospital equipment that was greatly needed for children suffering with this disease.

This became the pinnacle of Hefina's dressing up era! Every opportunity to don any form of costume was utilised. Dressing up and visiting all the pubs and clubs up and down the valley to collect as much as they could was the ultimate aim of the committee.

Between 1979 and 1985, Hefina was at the height of her committee involvement. She turned her attentions to the community she lived in and entered into a mission of supporting as many causes as she felt were deserving.

The Labour Party played a huge part in Hefina's life. She was a member of the Seven Sisters ward and never missed a meeting or campaign. She would deliver leaflets through doors and worked on the polling station when Election Day came around.

Hefina helped to fight for a community centre to be formed in the village. The old Pit Head Baths in Seven Sisters lay empty for many years. Hefina was part of the group responsible for turning it around. Whilst working on the venture, they were able to open a weekly disco for the children as well as film nights and events. There were also youth hostel facilities put into the rooms at the back of the centre. This was another major fundraising opportunity that Hefina thrived on.

* * *

At the bottom of Hefina's street was the ATC (Air Training Corps). Mr Ron Morris contacted Hefina and asked her if she would like to help them to fundraise and be part of the Civilian Committee. The responsibility of the committee was to manage the financial resources of the squadron. Money raised would provide activities such as annual camps and adventure training. It was part of the Number 3 Welsh Wing ATC Squadrons, a charitable organisation and a local club for the youngsters of the Dulais Valley.

Hefina played a major part in caring for the building for the ATC. She held a key to the premises and with Jayne's help she ran the tuck shop for the boys.

As a devoted member of Soar Chapel, attending every Sunday Hefina helped with the Christian Aid charity. This charity worked to fight international inequality and overcome poverty around the world. She also became the treasurer of the Cwmdulais Christian Fellowship which comprised of four chapels and churches in the village. These were Soar Chapel, St Mary's Church, Salem and Bethany Chapel.

During these years, the Playscheme was born, allowing children access to games and craft activites during the summer holidays. The Playscheme was held at 'the rec' (recreation ground) in Seven Sisters. They held a barbeque and fancy dress disco night and a sports day. The scheme was a success and carried on for many years. Hefina was one of the founder members of the Seven Sisters Playscheme and as Alison was training to be a nursery nurse, she encouraged her daughter to apply for a position one summer.

* * *

On 29th August, 1981 Alison married Russell Williams, Hefina was involved in organising the wedding, she made the bridesmaids dresses and arranged for the reception to be held at the Onllwyn Miners' Welfare. For a short while Alison and Russell lived with Hefina, John and Jayne. By December 1981 they had moved to their first home, a first floor flat in Onllwyn.

* * *

In the South Atlantic Ocean just off the coast of Argentina lay a small group of Islands called the Falklands owned by the British state. On 2nd April, 1982 Argentinean forces landed on the islands. By 5th April a task force was sent from Britain to liberate the islands, thus began the Falklands Conflict. By 21st May, British troops had landed and by 14th June, Argentina had surrendered. Not without its casualties, this war was short but brutal. Hefina was to suffer anxiety during this time as Ian was bound for the Falklands, thankfully his ship managed to avoid the heavy conflict. However, Ian's best friend Paddy was serving on HMS Ardent which sank, but Paddy survived and returned home safely. The news was rife with the conflict. Hefina had a map of the Falkland Islands (drawn from a newspaper article) on the wall above the fire place. With the help of her daughter Jayne, they made British and Argentinian flags from paper, sewing pins and glue. After each report she would move the flags to the areas of the Falklands taken by each side. Even though she could relax a little knowing Ian was safe, when it was over, it was a tremendous relief for Hefina.

* * *

PTA (Parent Teacher Association) and the board of Governors were organisations you would find Hefina part of during these years. Both the Welsh and English primary schools in the village and the Welsh comprehensive school in Ystalyfera all received her support and involvement.

Another organisation that received her support was the Dulais Valley Silver Band. The hall was situated at the top of Station Terrace in Seven Sisters. It was a tin shack building and had been there for decades. Jayne was a member of the band, therefore Hefina was a parent member of the committee, again using her skills to fundraise and be part of organising concerts. During the village carnivals the band would march through the streets with the drum section following. In June, 1982 they came first at the Welsh Miners' Gala competition which qualified them for the National Mineworkers (Fourth Section) competition in Blackpool in the November of that year. Off they went on the long journey up to the North of England. The band came 16th out of 16 bands entered. However, this didn't perturb them, every member and their families had the best time away.

* * *

This era would see Jennifer leaving the British Isles. She had spent many years working in London but had decided it was time to move on. She accepted a position with DFDS Seaways and headed for the American coast working on the cruise ships as a croupier.

On 16th November, 1983 Jennifer married Steven Vigue. This was a marriage of convenience; Steven was a gay man and Jennifer wanted to become a legal citizen of America, so she could remain working in the US.

* * *

Hefina was a very busy woman, her typical day consisted of getting up and going to the village. She would call into the Post Office, the Paper Shop and maybe one or two of the other shops for her groceries on her way to Canolfan to visit her mother and her Auntie Lil. It was very rare for her not to visit them each day.

She would be home by lunch (known as dinner time) to cook the main meal. This would usually be left on plates on top of saucepans filled with water and the pan lids on top of the food, for everyone to warm their meal if they weren't there at that time. These were the days before the microwave. Pebble Mill and Emmerdale Farm were her favourite TV programmes so these would be on whilst she cooked the food.

Hefina didn't deviate from the weekly menu too often, and could be very predictable about what was to be eaten each week. For instance:

Mon	Ham and parsley sauce
Tues	Faggots, peas and potatoes with Bovril gravy
Wed	Chicken roast dinner
Thur	Pork or lamb chops or liver and onions
Fri	Corned beef pasty or pie with chips from the Chip Shop
Sat	Free for all, eating whatever was available from the cupboard and always a mixture of cucumber in vinegar, beetroot, pickles, 'shibwns' (spring onions – this may be part of the strange 'Wenglish' dialect), radish and usually cold meat like tongue and sliced ham or corned beef
Sun	The infamous beef, lamb or pork roast dinner with home made thick Welsh gravy

On a Friday Hefina would visit her hairdresser, Diana, so she would not make food, instead everyone would be gathered at Canolfan to eat. Bread would be delivered from the Banwen Bakery and Hefina would always buy a white cob and cakes, her favourite being anything with fresh cream and custard slices! Late evenings would bring Agazis' Ices, who drove up the street at around 9pm. Hefina would buy a wafer ice cream for herself and a cone for Boomer the dog.

She would then have set routines for the week: her washing day was Monday where she would pull out her twin tub into the kitchen, fill it with water, attach the hose to the sink and wash and spin for hours, Tuesday was ironing day and Thursday was cleaning day. She would clean upstairs and down each week, dusting and vaccuming.

Nearly every evening would be taken up by a committee meeting of some type. She had a different briefcase or bag for each committee's paperwork and these would be lined up in the parlour ready to pick up and leave. On a Friday and Saturday Hefina and John would continue to frequent their favourite haunts for a pint of bitter and a gin and lemonade!

CHAPTER 6

Significant Differences

"You're twenty years too late. There's something the matter with you. You didn't come out on strike when they closed Seven Pit in 1964. You're mad. Why worry about the English pits? Worry more about the Welsh pits."

Hefina questioning John's beliefs when he came home announcing the strike of '84

The government announced on 6th March, 1984 its intention to close twenty coal mines, revealing the plan in the long-term to close over seventy pits in the UK. It was the 12th March, 1984. Mass walkouts and strikes began following this revelation undertaken by the National Union of Mineworkers (NUM) led by Arthur Scargill.

The Neath, Dulais and Swansea Valley Miners' Support Group was born on 21st April, 1984.

The strike had lasted longer than those in 1972, 1974 and 1981. Hefina now had the time to devote to the cause and jumped in with both feet. It was inevitable that she would be part of this group. To become secretary was the best role for her where she could utilise her skills.

In 1995 Hefina was interviewed by Mair Francis for her dissertation titled 'Women and the Aftermath of the 1984-85 Miners' Strike - A South Wales Analysis'. The following pages comprise of the personal diary of Hefina from April 1984 to December 1985 as presented to Mair.

"*Interviewee A (Hefina Headon) was the oldest of the women interviewed. She was 54 during the strike, married to a striking miner and a mother of four grown up children and she took on the responsibility of Secretary to the Support Group. Her role was to take minutes and report to every weekly meeting. She developed links with the Women Against Pit Closures and the Quarymen's Support Group in Blaenau Ffestiniog and was responsible in organising the 'Glorious Twelfth' celebrations which commemorated the beginning and the end of the strike; these were organised every year after the strike for seven years. As one of the pro-active members of the group she had close links with the gay and lesbian group, she also spoke on behalf of the Support Group at public meetings."*

The following pages are an amalgamation Hefina's diary and Support Group minutes during the strike.

The Diary 1984

6 May — Food parcels
The central pick up point is at Onllwyn Miners' Welfare Hall. Two ladies from each village meet at the welfare at 9:15am on Tuesday 8 May to make up bags and deliver to each centre. Centres open from 11am until 1pm Tuesday and Thursday.

Amount of food in each bag amounts to:

	Single Person	Families
Potatoes	3	8
Carrots	3	6
Peas	1 tin	1 tin
Meat	1 tin	1 tin
Bread	½ loaf	1 loaf
Baked Beans	1 tin	1 tin
Cereal	½ packet Weetabix	1 packet
Orange or Apple	1	1

12 May — Women from all over Britain met in Barnsley (10,000).

22 May	Women left for Cynheidre Colliery at 5:30am, were stopped by police 10 miles away and had to walk in the rain, we were picked up by miners going to picket, we joined them.
28 May	March and rally held at Pontyberem, I spoke in Welsh.
29 May	A women's meeting was held at Ammanford to discuss picketing.
12 June	A march and rally held in Cardiff, Tony Benn spoke.
15 June	A barbeque at Onllwyn Miners' Welfare Hall.
18 June	The battle of Orgreave.
23 June	Women lobbied Margaret Thatcher at Porthcawl. 23 turned up at 7am, we arrived at Porthcawl at 8am, we were first at the barriers, stood until 11:45am when Maggie arrived. 2 police cars accompanied her, she alighted from the car, walked straight into the pavilion without looking back, we shouted "Maggie, Maggie, Maggie, out, out, out!" Then at 12:45pm she came out and a farmer threw an egg and it caught her in the chest. She just wiped her hand over it and carried on into the car covered by an umberella, another egg was thrown and hit one of her security men.
27 June	A march and rally at Portsmouth, I spoke. The rally took place at the Guild Hall we marched to Alexander Park where the miners were picketing. The speakers and chairmen were Chairman of trades, SOGAR and Labour council. Banners displayed were South Wales Miners' who led the march. Also thanks to people of Portsmouth, Portsmouth Trades Council, SWP Branch and Labour Party, Kenwood AEUW and NUDE Area No 1. On the return journey we called at

Greenham Common and chatted to the women and saw the conditions they lived in and the way the base was guarded by the police and how the base was fenced off by a 20 foot barbed wire fence.

29 June	Barbeque held at Kingfisher in Crynant.
4 July	We met women in Swansea who wanted to support us.
6 July	Six of our women went to meetings held in Blaenau Ffestiniog, North Wales.
13 July	A barbeque was held in the Miners' Welfare Hall in Seven Sisters.
17 July	We met the men from the N.G.A. Union in London, they came down every fortnight with cash for us.
18 July	Women's first meeting in Cardiff. Women came from Cwm Rhymney Valley, Ammanford, Hirwaun, Oakdale, Mardy, Abertillery, Cardiff, Reading, Newbridge, Penrhiwceiber, Mountain Ash and Greenham Common. The women proposed a walk, to unite at one point, this should take 4 or 5 day. Topics discussed: storing nuclear waste in closed pits, non union workers in power stations. Walk 10 miles a day, raise money for transport, NUM solicitors helped, arrested women, G leaflet will be printed about the nights women have with the police.
20 July	A barbeque held at Glynneath Rugby Club, met Nicolas Bell from France, arranged for children to spend a holiday.
24 July	Went picketing in Margam.
27 July	Eight Women went to stay in Ambergate Derby and attended meeting.

30 July	Miners' trip to Oxwich.
3I July	Extraordinary meeting with bank manager, our money sequestrated, we got it all.
I August	Trip to Porteynon.
9 August	Three miners and myself attended a meeting at Llandrindod Wells (Theatre Powys).
II August	Mass Women's March in London, laid black roses at No. I0 Downing Street. Women went from support group, arrived in London, march started at I2pm. Speakers were Joy Fletcher, Jo Richardson MP, Vice President of GLC and others. Started walking at Ipm. 20,000 women walked down Whitehall and they laid black flowers with messages written on every flower, all filed past I0 Downing Street in silence. A gas bill for millions of pounds was handed into the DHSS office at Elephant and Castle to represent the benefits that were withheld from miners' families. Mrs Ann Scargill and Mrs Betty Heathfield handed a 20,000 signatures petition into Buckingham Palace, appealing to the Queen, she at least expressed some concern, it read "The women of British mining communities appeal for your support, we ask your Majesty to speak on our behalf."
I8 August	March and rally held in Neath.
3I August	Picketing in Margam, I02 men took over a rig, another group of men took over Transport bridge at Llanwern, Newport.
I September	Women's march at Beddau, one minute silence held outside scabs house.
3 September	Coach full went to lobby T.U.C. Conference

34

	at Brighton, 2 planes with banners stating 'Privatise Unions, Get stuffed SCARGILL'.
8 September	Three coaches went to Barbeque at Hay Castle.
14 October	Crynant Male Voice Choir gave a Concert at Onllwyn Miners' Welfare Hall.
19 October	Supported miners at Port Talbot Court, case adjourned.
21 October	Support group meeting discussed LGSM visit, Margaret reported that the accommodation for the gays and lesbians arriving next weekend had all been arranged. 30 of them coming down.
22 October	I spoke to Swansea University students.
23 October	I spoke to Age Concern.
27 October	March and rally at Swansea, Country and Western held at Onllwyn. Met lesbian and gay men.
1 November	Attended a meeting with Theatre Powys, they offered a pantomime for the children.
8 November	Picket meeting at Pyle, women asked to take over the Cynheidre Pit Head Baths on 9th November. Students arrived from Harrow.
9 November	Conference held in Sheffield. Attended WAPC. Conference at Chesterfield with three other women, stayed at Cricket Club, pickets looked after us, kept press away. On the way home I was chosen to speak at a rally on 13 November.
13 November	On the platform of the Afan Lido with Arthur Scargill, Peter Heathfield and Mick McGahey. I was very proud and spoke well, 6,000 people

	attended, I had a standing ovation.
14 November	Picketed our local collieries.
18 November	Seventeen women took over the manager's office at Cynheidre for 5 days and nights, broke up all the furniture and windows, nothing was said about it.
	Report given by Edwina Roberts: The women climbed into the manager's office at 11:30pm (sixteen women), the under manager found out next morning, and said "Not that Seven again!" They shouted abuse to the scabs passing under the window and at 2:30pm they returned. Next day police drove them around the back way. Another woman arrived. The only mistake made, they only took over the top floor which was filthy dirty, they should have taken over the whole block. They did so on Wednesday at 4:30pm by tricking the manager. They locked him out. They shouted 'scab' when they were going to the shower and one man exposed himself. Police were shouting "Double pay! Double pay!" then they cut the electric off, then the gas went out. Told on Thursday they would be there until Sunday, only 12 women left. They were told there were 66 scabs but they only counted 57. They received 2 letters, one with a box of chocolates. Edwina finished by saying "They need help in Cynheidre and I don't mean food!"
20 November	Picketed Abernant, asked the manager why he sent back-to-work letters to the men, he said he was doing his job.
26 November	Picketed DHSS offices, Neath.
27 November	Coach full of women sang and beat a drum outside 'Strikebreaker 1's' home (a known scab), police

arrived, Women History Group did a video, went to friend's house (Janet) for tea, police stayed with us the whole time, we then attended Wales Congress meeting at Pontyberem.

29 November   Wales Congress Rally at Gwyn Hall, Neath, Ystradgynlais Male Voice Choir sang, I spoke.

4 December   Sian James and I went to London, spoke to Brent NALGO Polytec Student Teachers meeting, Striking Miners' Choir performed a concert at Hornesey, I spoke.

8 December   March and rally at Cardiff with Ann Scargill, I spoke.

10 December   Back to London, minibus full attended the Bronski Beat Concert (Pits & Perverts).
Minibus full went to London to the Bronski Beat benefit show on Monday 10 December by lesbians and gays. Wonderful welcome, lovely vegetarian meal prepared at the Fallen Angel. David and Hefina spoke, the audience were very appreciative. Everyone enjoyed themselves. David brought £8,000 back that week. The lesbians made a fuss of me. A miner's wife from Kiverton Park cried and begged, a bucket was sent around the hall and she had £1,000 to take home.

14 December   Flying Pickets did a show at the Parc and Darc Hall, Betty Heathfield spoke and the women who took over Cynheidre Colliery were presented.

14 December   Trip to London.
May was in charge of 50 children on a coach to London for the weekend. The coach broke down for 1½ hours, stopped at Aust Services. Arrived Brent Town Hall at 5pm, no one to meet us, no one knew anything. We were taken into buildings, given

37

squash and coffee and they phoned around, found out it was Westminster Town Hall. Mr Dai Davies formerly of Treorchy volunteered to show us the way and arrived there at 7pm. We were met by GLC chairman Illtyd Harrington and Ken Livingstone. The spread laid out for the children was lovely, they all received a carrier bag full of goodies from West Ham Football Club. The hosts came to meet us.

Saturday everyone did something different, then disco and buffet again, left at 1:30pm on Sunday. Every child received a lovely hamper of food, and May received a cheque for £500 from Brent Labour Party. The people of Brent had high praise for all the children and asked if they could stay longer. An elderly lady approached May and gave her 2 carrier bags full of food, and they used them on the way home. The trip was a great success.

21 December	Every miner had a turkey, parties everywhere.
29 December	A scab meeting being held in Pendine, no meeting. Coach full went to Pendine to scab meeting, arrived at meeting, people keeping Beach Hotel were unsociable, coach driver unreasonable, if he had known it wasn't a sponsored swim, he would not have driven the coach! Edwina had such a shock she asked him if he drove scabs to work, he refused to answer, he also refused to take us to 'Strikebreaker 1's' house (a known scab) and threatened if he dropped us at 'Strikebreaker 2' (another known scab) he would go back to the garage!

The Diary: 1985

3 January	Belgian visitors brought money.
22 January	Mass picket at Treforgan 1 scab.

24 January	Met Kath Jones at Port Talbot, £1,736 given to the children.
25 January	Seven women went to Nottingham. Hefina and Sian along with a few others arrived at University College Campus in Nottingham and had lunch. We picketed at the colliery, only 9 police men on duty, the miners asked us not to shout at the miners going to work because they were giving leaflets asking them to keep in the NUM. We gave them some food. There was a hut used by pickets but the police had boarded it up. 2 women living close by acted as prostitutes to the police. Hefina spoke at the meeting at Ollerton Welfare Club. We were there to hear what the Notts people had to say (if you scab you help Thatcher!) We were given badges and mugs, four depressed people came back with us.
27 January	Scarlett Harletts perfom at the Onllwyn Welfare Hall. A women's theatre group from London, they came and performed a play on rape for us.
11 February	I spoke with Sian on the same platform as Dennis Skinner MP, people in London very bitter about Maggie.
13 February	I spoke to first year students at Newport College.
14 February	Went out at 3am to picket at Nantgarw, Tower and Treforgan collieries. Picketed Blaenant colliery.
18 February	Nine women went to Ilkeston Nottingham. Dave Jones killed on picket line.
19 February	Meeting held in Walthamstow, London, Sian and I spoke. Met with the Scarlett Harletts.

2I February	March and rally in Cardiff with Ann Scargill.
26 February	Return to work call, lobby the miners at Crynant.
I March	Nottingham women and lesbian and gay men visited at Coelbren Club. Meeting Porthcawl. Back to work.
8 March	International Women's Day.
9 March	Wales Congress held in London, invited to Woolwich for a meal, concert held by striking miners. Gays held a jumble sale.
II March	Met Kath Jones, £849 given for the children.
I2 March	First reunion held at Onllwyn Miners' Welfare Club, it was a huge success, we had to lock the doors at 9 o'clock as the place was packed, we decided to hold it annually.
I5 March	'Angry Summer' play at Onllwyn Welfare.
I6 March	Van donated by lesbian and gay men £2,500. The Lesbian and Gay Men Support the Miners group logo was discussed. The women insisted that the logo be painted on the van. Sian believed it was a statement of our thanks and commitment to LGSM. When it was proposed it was not instantly agreed. Indeed, there was some reluctance to paint the van. This led to a discussion, mainly from men, they hid behind the excuse that by painting the logo on the doors and 'branding' the van then the re-sale value would be reduced. This was a potential £200. As we had no intention of selling the van, the women felt that it was an unnecessary argument and insisted it was painted. It was not part of the deal with LGSM and not requested by them. They were very moved by our decision and fully recognised that it was the women who wanted

	this tangible recognition of LGSM's generosity and a public acknowledgement of their support.
20 March	Last strike parcel today.
23 March	Harrow Old Thyme Music Hall held a show for us.
30 March	Eight of us invited to Dirty Thirty reunion in Leicester.
I April	Children invited out to Germany and Belgium.
24 April	Meeting held to discuss Support Group, made resolution to help people in need.
2 May	Paul Robeson Junior met us in Onllwyn.
4 May	May Day Rally in Portsmouth and Southampton, I spoke.
7 May	Mass picket in court, jailed miners.
9 May	Sian James elected chairperson South Wales Women.
25 May	First Women's Day school at Onllwyn.
I June	Wales Congress Conference at Maesteg.
I5 June	Striking Miners' Choir sang at concert in London, Mark Ashton spoke. I2 from Support Group went.
I8 June	I02 miners in Crown Court, Swansea.
22 June	First South Wales Women's conference held in Aberdare.
29 June	Invited to the Gay Pride march held in London, what a sight!
I July	Theatre Powys did a play for us.
II July	Went up to Houses of Parliament.

13 July	Barbeque at Hay Castle.
10 August	National Eisteddfod at Rhyl, I thanked everyone for their support.
17 August	Second WAPC conference at Sheffield.
14 September	Imogen our friendly photographer gave an exhibition in London.
16 September	Helped the pickets at NUR dispute in Pyle.
24 September	Sent cheque and letter of support to Blaenau Ffestiniog Quarry.
30 September	Lobbied Labour Party conference at Bournemouth. Set up DOVE Workshop for women.
2 November	March and rally at Blaenau Ffestiniog, Sian spoke, gave out lamps and badges.
8 November	Met unions that supported us in Ostend.
14 November	Concert held at Onllwyn Miners' Welfare Hall for Blaenau Quarry Strikers.
20 December	Took food and toys up to Blaenau Ffestiniog.
22 December	Support group get together. Supported Brent NALGO in their dispute. Also sang Silent Night.

* * *

In this two year period, Hefina would be the busiest she had ever experienced. As she was never at home, she used to leave notes for the family with instuctions, like the note she left one night for John which read:

"TURN LIVER AND CHOPS OVER. Take liver out first, chop on its own to be cooked the most."

Notes were also left for her, like this one left by Jayne:

"Auntie Rona has got flu, she won't be down this weekend!"

This is how life was during the strike.

On 13th November, 1984 Hefina was asked to speak at the Afon Lido, Aberafon at the Strike Support Rally. She stood on the podium alongside Arthur Scargill, President of the NUM, his Vice President Mr Mick McGahey and General Secretary Mr Peter Heathfield. On the back of a photograph taken by the South Wales Evening Post Hefina wrote "My Claim to Fame".

The following day an article appeared in the South Wales Evening Post News, titled 'Rally Success Overwhelming'. 6500 people turned up, *"It was estimated that as many as 1,000 people failed to get into the sports centre where the corridors, balconies and gaps between the seats were jammed with miners."* This article continues *"But one of the biggest ovations was for Mrs Edwina* (they got her name incorrect) *Headon, of the South Wales Miners' Wives Support Group. Mrs Headon, from Llanelli* (also incorrect) *spoke of tremendous support from the vast majority of pitmen's wives at Cynheidre Colliery for the strike."*

This was her rousing speech that day:

My name is Hefina Headon

By birth a miner's daughter

By design a miner's wife

By choice a Socialist

I am secretary to Neath, Dulais and Swansea Valley Miners' Support Group.

We have the best support group in South Wales, it is made up of seven villages and two towns, we make 1100 parcels a week, we work very hard raising money and due to contacts and twinnings, and thanks to you good people

43

we will survive.

Twenty years ago the NCB closed twelve pits in our valley alone, there's no industry in my village since then.

I have been asked what is our aim? Jobs, jobs for the future generations.

The solidarity we experience in South Wales is far from what the people in Nottingham are facing, having visited them, the misery the working miners cause, and the police state that exists there.

This is a woman's fight as well as a man's, and now the women have shown they are a force to be reckoned with, getting up at 3am to go on the picket lines side by side with the miners.

I salute colleagues of mine who took over the managers' office at the pit head baths for five days and nights.

Certainly no one will be able to say again that women are a conservative force in the working class – we have been liberated, new energies which cannot be suppressed again and it has been fantastic to be part of it all.

We have a lot to thank this strike for. We have emerged stronger and more determined as people, and we are strengthened as a community. Perhaps when this is all over the contribution which the women have made will be seen as a truly crucial factor in this struggle.

After the strike we will have to find somewhere to channel our energy. Most of us will never sit at home again.

We women are kind and generous but are called the 'Enemy Within'. We are fighting for communities and the future.

It's marvellous what mutual hardship can bring out in people. Our union and communities have been built through struggle and sacrifice over a long period. It is our task to defend them so that we may hand them on to the next generation.

In this strike the struggle was directly against the NCB and pit closures. A blow to the miners is a blow to all the working classes.

Trade union democracy has been fought for, developed and refined over 150 years. The courts are being used more and more as a means to attack trade unions. The courts have taken over the decision as to when a strike is official. If the union refuses to abide by the decision, then its funds are seized by sequesters and receivers, so that it is powerless to act for its members.

Stand by your principles, stand by your union, save your jobs and communities.

To our friends who have supported us financially and morally in our struggle, I say to you:

They tried to starve us out, you were there.
We needed food donations, you were there.
We needed strength on demonstrations, you were there.
When we needed help to picket, you were there.
Whatever help or task, we only had to ask.
We need not have worried, you were there.

Maggie tried to tell us you weren't there.
Oh! Where could they be looking?
What did they think they were cooking?
You certainly showed them you were there.
Words can't express our thanks for being there.
We will always remember you being there,
and if ever you need us you only have to call,

as we can guarantee we'll be there.

Diolch

Christmas wasn't far off and the families were worrying about how they would be celebrating that year. Traditional Christmas dinner was not even considered, but that was about to change. The Welsh Labour Party group was to donate £500 to the Miners' Support Group to make sure that every striking miner had a turkey at Christmas. This was announced by MP Mr Donald Coleman at a rally in support of the miners in the Gwyn Hall, Neath on 29th November, 1984.

There was plenty of food on the table that Christmas and due to donations of presents and clothes for the children, there seemed to be enough under the little Christmas tree. The small plastic tree which was looking a bit worn and tired, stood taller than usual this year, as the family was able to celebrate during these hard times.

Food parcels were to become the norm during the strike. They usually consisted of a range of items, some were not what people were used to but were greatly appreciated none the less. There were tins of stewed steak and tinned potatoes, tinned meats and mushy peas. Loaves of bread and potatoes were also staples of the parcels and were packed in boxes or plastic carrier bags. These were allocated to every family. Food and clothes turned up from everywhere and in abundance.

There were so many clothes, it was decided that a 'Nearly New' shop would be opened. This was first held at the ATC hut in Seven Sisters and later moved to the old Chemist Shop in the village centre. It was open each morning and volunteers from the support group managed the shop. Clothes were sent from all over the world and sold for a moderate sum in the shop. They sold everything ranging from baby clothes to men's trousers, women's shoes, coats, jackets and even underwear!

When Hefina told her mother and her Auntie Lil (who was an esteemed embroiderer) that she was planning on making a banner for the support group, Auntie Lil offered her services. She made a lovely embroidered centre piece for the wheel in the banner. With the help of her family, Hefina cut out, sewed and embroidered the banner which was to become the famous banner of the support group.

At the begining of the strike, Ian had announced that he would be marrying his fiancé, Jackie Shipp. They had planned for the wedding to take place in Jackie's hometown of Portsmouth in August, 1984. Ian didn't expect any help from his mother and father, however, Hefina being the organiser that she was, arranged for a coach full of family and friends to attend the wedding.

There was also to be another member of the family born during the strike. Alison gave birth to Daniel in February, 1985. Her husband Russell was a striking miner and times were extremely hard for them, but Hefina made sure that they wanted for nothing and welcomed Daniel into the world.

Another new beginning was also to unfold during this struggle. The idea of the DOVE Workshop was born. DOVE – Dulais Opportunities for Voluntary Enterprise – This idea had derived from discussions had by Mair Francis and Kay Bowen and others from the support group.

> *"The group met for meetings and classes in members' homes, until they were able to use an old derelict billiard hall in Onllwyn. Subsequent to an unsuccessful bid for a grant from 'Opportunities for Volunteering' in November 1984, an application was made again in March 1985 and a grant of £600 was obtained in September 1985 to cover volunteer fees to establish a machine knitting co-operative and a community launderette".*

Mair Francis – Up The DOVE (2008) p9

Hefina was a member of the organising committee of the DOVE workshop along with Mair Francis, Kay Bowen, Julie Rees, Marilyn James, Letty Jenkins, Christine Marshall, Janet Thomas, Irene Craddock, Sonia Wheeler, Carys Davies, Mair Bennett and Susan Harris. The workshop secured new grants and were able to move forward to premises of their own and employ members of staff whilst building courses for the community. They offered a crèche facility for the children and a café to name a few.

Hefina's busy calendar was to continue from here on in, supporting organisations and meeting new people, travelling far and wide. New missions were afoot!

CHAPTER 7

Rolling Along

1st January, 1986 *"Happppyyyyy New Year!!!"* Hefina raises a glass to John at the Onllwyn Inn, *"What is going to happen this year I wonder?"*

Hefina's daily and weekly routines were stabilised again. Life was getting back to normal as normal as it could ever be. The DOVE workshop was well on its way and other projects were popping up within the community to take up Hefina's time, such as the community centre. It still had much to do in the way of development and Hefina spent time weekly at the centre ensuring all was well. The youth discos were a regular occurrence and raised funds to sustain themselves.

Her new calendar that appeared on the wall of the kitchen each year was already filled with birthdays and events planned for months in advance.

John was now coming up to his retirement. He decided he would remain with Long's Buses and work for them. John and Hefina enjoyed trips away over the weekends. She would sometimes encourage and persuade her mother Katie and Auntie Lil to go away and enjoy life while they could, but Katie was always reluctant. She was now in a wheelchair and her pernicious anemia had taken hold of her. Lil was a spinster who lived for her embroidery and even in her 90s she was still capable of sitting at her canvas and creating wonderful landscapes.

Cae Mawr (the street in which Hefina lived) was a small cul-de-sac. Everyone knew each other and there was a strong community spirit within the street. The children would knock on the door and come straight in with "Can I play?" Hefina never refused. They played both out in the garden and inside with the toys she kept, and the children chatted to her about everything. Hefina also seemed to attract dogs! Herself and John owned many dogs throughout their married life. Whilst in Onllwyn they had terrier mongrels that no one else wanted, Rusty and then Mick. When they moved to Seven Sisters, the Tuckers who lived next door had a dog called Sooky. She took a liking to Hefina's and spent most of her days in front of the fire until she would be sent home at night. When Sooky died they decided to have another dog of their own. In 1984 they bought Boomer, a Spaniel Labrador cross breed; Hefina never walked the dogs, nor did she bother with them much, but they still loved her.

* * *

Jennifer came home from America on a short visit in January, 1986 to celebrate Jayne's 18th birthday. She met Alison's baby Daniel for the first time and brought presents for everyone. She was greatly missed when she was away for such long periods; she had not been back for two years but she was soon gone again by the end of the month.

* * *

Another new addition joined the family in April, 1986. Christopher was born to Ian and Jackie. This was Hefina's second grandson. She and John went to visit the family in Portsmouth where they had now settled. She adored her children and her grandchildren. This was evident in the topics of discussion with her friends and the photos she kept of everyone in her handbags.

* * *

Jayne left home to join the British Army in July, 1986. It was a very difficult time for Hefina. Margaret Thatcher was still in government and she resented Jayne working for 'them', but she also understood that there was no future for Jayne in the valleys and leaving would open up new horizons for her, as they did for Ian. They waved goodbye at Neath train station as she made her way to Guildford for basic training with the Women's Royal Army Corps.

Just as Hefina was settling down to life with John at home, and looking after Daniel for Alison, tragedy struck Hefina once again. It was July, 1986 when a call came through from America. Jennifer had been involved in a motorbike accident in Reno, Nevada at 5am that morning on her way home from work. She was travelling as a pillion passenger on her boss' motorbike. They hit a wall and Jennifer received multiple head injuries and fell into a coma. She tragically passed away five hours later. Hefina was understandably inconsolable.

Just a few days later it was Jayne's passing out parade in Guildford. The family travelled there and met at the barracks. They had decided not to inform Jayne until after the parade. It was an extremely sad day for the whole family. They had lunch in Guildford town centre before heading home. During Jayne's compassionate leave, the lounge at the Conolfan flats held a memorial service for Jennifer. The service was beautiful and there were many tears shed by all. Hefina seemed as though her heart had been ripped from her chest.

Jennifer's ashes were to remain in the US. Her favourite place was Portland, Maine, on the East Coast of America. She enjoyed her respite and recuperation there after her hysterectomy and had told her family how beautiful it was. Jennifer's friends scattered her ashes into the Maine river. It was extremely difficult for everyone in the family to accept Jennifer's passing. Without a body to lay to rest it was a very strange experience. Hefina tried to seek solace in attending medium evenings and spiritual churches to find any hint of answers to her long list of questions. The only piece of consistent information they were able to give her was that she was accompanied by a small brown and white Jack Russell Terrier dog spirit. Hefina believed this to be one of her previous dogs, Mick!

Her grief distanced her from her close family. She cut herself off from physical affection and would not speak about Jennifer. This was the last child from her first marriage to be cruelly taken away from her.

Hefina, without fail, visited her mother and Auntie Lil daily. On occasions when she was unable to visit, she would arrange for her niece, Monica or Diana (Hefina's hair dresser) to take care of them, even though they also received home care and a cleaner. Both Katie and Lil were also extremely distraught over Jennifer's death, as she had lived with them as a child at Tan-y-Coed and was particularly close to both.

As Hefina dealt with her own grief independently, Jayne decided to return to her Army training in Yorkshire and was later posted to Germany to serve with the Royal Signal Regiment. John and Hefina visited her on a few occasions and enjoyed the time as well as they could.

September, 1986 Hefina was brought her third grandson, Alex, born to Russell and Alison. This helped to distract her from her grief. She was more than happy to look after Daniel and Alex for Alison and between her and John they managed to still make time for her to attend all her meetings and classes. Russell was a miner and by now had been made redundant when they closed Blaenant Colliery. He had to retrain and attended the DOVE Workshop to gain new employability skills.

With Hefina out of the house most of the time, it was inevitable that it would become neglected. The woodchip on the walls was looking tired. The Parkray coal fire had seen its day and a large Rayburn cooker was fitted in its place. Hefina loved to cook huge roast dinners on the Rayburn. The home was always very warm and cosy despite Hefina's tendency to hoard! Clutter was a permanent fixture at number 19.

Shoes and matching handbags were Hefina's vice. She had a set for every outfit. The catalogue was her favourite method of shopping - she was far too busy to visit the town. She had an account with 'Marshall Ward'. Shoes would randomly arrive at the home on a monthly basis. They filled the space beneath her double bed. Court shoes were her favourite style, although she would wear flats on occasions. She didn't own a pair of trainers or a pair of wellington boots. When gardening she would don a pair of Ian's old 1970s platform shoes, orange and brown leather, and off she would go!

Hefina was still heavily involved as a socialist and remained involved in different groups supporting causes. Paul Robeson Junior, a human rights speaker and son of the famous American actor of the same name visited the valleys in March, 1989. He was undertaking a lecture tour of Britain where he was invited to the Swansea College. He met up with Hywel Francis (head of the college's adult education department and former chair of the Neath, Dulais and Swansea Valley Miners' Support Group).

Three years earlier, she had met Paul when he visited for the first time. Hefina enjoyed the musicals and especially Riverboat (1936) in which Paul Robeson Senior sang 'Ol' Man River'. Paul gave her a copy of the funeral sevice booklet from his father's funeral in 1976 as a gift.

* * *

In 1989, Jayne married Stuart Meldrum, a Scottish soldier who also serving with the Royal Signals. They met in Germany and later married in August at Soar Chapel. Hefina made the bridesmaids dresses as she did for Alison and Russell's wedding, she also made her own outfit. As Jayne and Stuart were living abroad, Hefina planned the whole event for them.

Routines were still part of her life, predictably she would be at Diana's the hairdressers every Friday morning without fail. She would gather with her friend Edwina, later joined by her sister in law Mary, gossiping and laughing. Hefina always had her hair coloured each month. Her hair style didn't change throughout her adulthood.

During 1990 Hefina decided to join the bowls team. A group of ladies from the village joined the local team together. Hefina was extremely good for a newcomer and had found something else to fill her life with. John spent hours waiting in cars for Hefina to finish; she was always the last to leave the room!

Prior to John and Hefina celebrating their 40th Wedding Anniversary, whilst walking home from the surgery, Hefina stepped over the cellar doors of the 'Bryn' pub in the lower part of the village and fell through breaking her ankle. This saw her with a cast on her leg and six weeks out of playing bowls.

* * *

The 90s brought plenty of political activity to Hefina's life, supporting Peter Hain into parliament and visiting London in April 1991 with her banner, showing solidarity and commitment to the Labour Party. They also visited Strazburg in July, 1992 with David Morris the Euro MP. This was later followed by another visit to the Jubilee Rooms in parliament in June, 1994.

With all three remaining children now married, it was inevitable that the family would grow and without a doubt it did. In April, 1993 Ian and Jackie had their second son, Mathew. Soon after in September, 1993 Jayne and Stuart had their second son, Sean (their first son Aaron was stillborn the previous year). Again Hefina made sure she was with the newborns as soon as she could. Ian and Jackie took Mathew to see Hefina and a few months later she jumped on a plane to Belfast to visit Sean in Northern Ireland.

Not long after Sean was born, Auntie Lil passed away peacefully in her sleep at the magnificent age of 98. Life would become quite lonely for Katie now and so Hefina made sure she spent more time with her mother and ensured others did too. The family were very close, Tommy and Katie had taken Hefina in when she was abandoned and abused by her first husband Johnny Smith. They had helped care for her children and were there when her son David died. She made sure she was there for her mother as a thank you for all she had done for her in the past.

More grandchildren were to come, and in February, 1996 Owen was born, another son to Jayne and Stuart. A year later Ashley was born in February, 1997 the last child for Ian and Jackie. Finally in August, 1998 Gregg was born, he would be the last son to Jayne and Stuart. Hefina now had eight grandsons, whom she was extremely proud of.

However, as usual, when there are good times, they are followed by bad. Katie passed away in November, 1996. She became unwell and was admitted to hospital where she died. This was another grief filled period for Hefina, who along with her family got through once again.

By 1997, Jayne was living in Cyprus. Whilst Alison and the family were out visiting, death would take another member of the family. This time, on the same day as Princess Diana, Hefina's niece Tessa died.

Tessa was Verona's second child, and Hefina found herself consoling Verona, empathising with her grief and loss. The family believed Tessa's death was due to the negligence of the second hospital that Tessa was transferred to for treatment, who instead of treating her for Meningitis gave her medication for a migraine. By the time they had noticed their error Tessa had died of the Meningitis infection. The family were on a mission, Ombudsmen were contacted and Verona fought for the negligence of the doctor involved to not go unnoticed. This would be a long battle but Hefina stuck by her side. Sadly it was never resolved. Verona's husband Tommy had passed away many years before and she was alone. Tessa had lived nearby with her two children, Sara and Jonathan, having gone through a messy divorce herself. Verona and Tessa always had each other for support.

Verona had become Mayoress of Chepstow in the early 90s and Tessa was her right hand woman. Hefina and Verona had much in common and would spend hours on the phone or face to face putting the world to rights. They visited Cyprus together after Tessa's passing, staying with Jayne and the family trying to relax and take respite away together.

Hefina enjoyed spending time with her grandchildren. In the village was a saw mills owned by the Tancocks, friends of Hefina's from her childhood. They had built an attraction called 'Gun Smoke', a mini western style theme park. Children could have guns made from wood and dress up as cowboys. There was plenty to do and see as they were growing up, and Hefina made sure they seized every opportunity.

The children were growing up, Jayne and the two boys had returned from Cyprus to live with Hefina and John, so that Gregg was born in Wales. During this time, John's health deteriorated. Jayne had found him collapsed on a few occasions. On one particular day she collected him from the 'Double H' club. He was sat outside on the bench covered in blood. John would cough until he passed out, and this had happened on the gravel. She helped him into the car and when they got home, he remained outside on the wall whilst Jayne cleaned up his face. Hefina used to get cross with him for drinking during the day when he wasn't well. He suffered with emphysema. At this time he had an electric nebuliser machine at home and he hooked himself up to it whilst rolling a cigarette! Typical John!

Jayne left to live in Northern Ireland in early October. Unbeknownst to the family, John had also developed lung cancer. This was diagnosed in October, 1998. They had decided between them to keep this from the family until it could no longer be a secret. John's treatment led him downhill rapidly. He was unable to eat and was later admitted to hospital. By late March, 1999 John left this life and Hefina was again to grieve the loss of the love of her life, her best friend and companion.

By the August of that year, Hefina would experience her own ill health. Alison had been at the house as usual, where Hefina had told her she was feeling unwell complaining of a sore left arm. Alison dropped her mother at the surgery thinking nothing more of it. That afternoon she went back to see how things had gone. Alison couldn't find Hefina and thinking that she may be at a meeting, saw to the dog Ken, then went home. By 9pm that evening Alison was still worried that her mother had not returned home and started to call around the three local hospitals. Hefina was found at Penrhywtyn Hospital. She had been admitted with a heart attack and the surgery had sent her to hospital immediately. Her sister Norma and her sister-in-law Mary were in hospital at the same time with heart problems.

Hefina's heart attack brought her sister Verona down from Chepstow to look after her. She began rehabilitation, participating in cardio exercise such as swimming. She also continued playing bowls. During this time she applied for a provisional driving license, even though driving was a skill she had never mastered in the past. When she attended the day surgery for a check up, her heart showed no signs of a heart attack. Thankfully she had managed to recover so well, she continued to walk everywhere, attending meetings and never failed to continue her community work. A stalwart to the core.

She was 69 years old.

CHAPTER 8

A Grand Finale

It was the first day of the new millennium: 1st January, 2000. Ian, Jackie, Christopher, Mathew and Ashley were all down from Portsmouth to spend new years day with Hefina.

Alison had been down in the morning to help her mother with dinner. Before hand Hefina had been to the bathroom several times to be sick. Alison asked her if she was ok, she replied she had a tummy bug. Everyone sat down for dinner but Hefina left the table a few times. Alison noticed she was still vomiting. She asked her again "Are you alright Mammy?" Hefina told Alison she had something caught in her throat and this made her sick.

Alison, Russell, Daniel and Alex left to go home and took Christopher with them. At around 6pm Alison received a call from Ian, he thought their mother was going into a diabetic hypoglycemia. She advised him to call the ambulance.

Jackie noticed that Hefina hadn't been herself all day. She sat down with her eyes closed. Hefina told Ian that she couldn't see anything. "I feel ever so strange, I feel giddy" she said. Suspecting she may have low blood sugar, Ian checked but the results were fine. He gave his mother a glass of water but she suddenly became violently sick. They called an ambulance. Ian accompanied Hefina while Alison followed on in the car. The paramedics checked Hefina's heart but that too was fine. He sought out the doctor on the ward who informed him that Hefina was drunk. She kept laughing and saying "This is silly, take me home, I dont want to stay here". This made everyone very cross. Many hours passed, when at around 1am, a consultant arrived who confirmed she had suffered a stroke.

Hefina spent six weeks in hospital. The family, advised by Verona, demanded they carried out MRI scans, as they noticed there was something wrong with her eyes. She was walking on her heels because she wasn't able to balance. Before Alison was willing for her to come home, she wanted tests to be carried out to confirm what kind of a stroke she had suffered. Once the MRI scan results came back, they were able to confirm she had a brain stem stroke which had affected the optic nerve. The stroke had severely damaged Hefina's sight. Her left eye would now see four fold. Hefina was advised to wear frosted glass in her glasses and she chose a blue glass. She didn't like wearing them especially when having a photograph taken and she would take them off for these occasions.

Whilst Hefina was in hospital, Alison and Jayne prepared the house for her return. Things had to change now she could no longer go upstairs. Luckily there was a downstairs toilet although it would be a while before she could use it properly. They cleared the parlour of all its clutter and decorated. They brought in a single bed, a TV and cabinet along with a small wardrobe for her clothes and a commode for her convenience. They also made sure the kitchen was cleared as she would be very unsteady on her feet.

Once Hefina returned home, she needed additional care. She attended Cimla hospital for rehabilitation. Alison and Verona fought for the home care service to visit Hefina. This took a while to sort out but eventually she was deemed eligible. They began their care plan, although, as stubborn and independent as she was, she wouldn't let them carry out half the tasks they were supposed to.

Jayne had moved back to England by this time. Not long after Hefina had settled down at home, she developed a water infection which led to her incontinence. This was another frustration for her to deal with. She constantly asked "Why me? Why did this have to happen to me?" Did this thwart her? Hell no, not Hellfire! Even though she couldn't walk without aid, she could only see with one eye, suffered incontinence and felt quite poorly at times with diabetes, she still managed to make her way to committee meetings and events.

* * *

Meanwhile, the DOVE Workshop had been continually improving. Grants and funding were accessed and partnerships were established. Hefina being so proud of the DOVE, still made sure she was part of the team. Hefina is photographed in the book, "Up the DOVE" written by Mair Francis. She supported all new aspects of this very successful enterprise and remained proud of all those involved, especially Mair.

Ironically, Hefina joined the 'Over 40s Club'. Finding that she was not able to physically carry out her community work as well as before, she still needed to go out and socialise.

Hefina was always a creative person, sewing and knitting were her past time favourites. She could no longer sew either by hand or with a machine so she turned her attention to knitting. In the days of her youth, she was taught to knit by her father and enjoyed it. Annually, John would acquire a new 'tossle hat' (without the 'tossle') and the grandchildren would also have hats and jumpers knitted for them. Hefina loved a particular knitted clown series, and planned a knitting marathon! There were builders and painters, gardeners and Christmas clowns and many more. She would also knit dolls and other toys. She used to knit without looking whilst watching television.

Another hobby of hers was doing crosswords. Hefina had a passion for them. She would have an old dictionary that belonged to her father and a thesaurus on the table. The books would be falling apart but she would battle her way through. Her favourite magazine at this time was 'Chat', a weekly glossy filled with real life stories and plenty of crosswords.

On Tuesdays, Hefina would visit Trem-y-Glyn. This was a respite care home where she would have a shower and spend time with others sitting watching television, chatting and knitting. They would have a meal there before coming home in the afternoon in the ambulance. Hefina made a few new friends at Trem-y-Glyn.

The 'Lifeline alarm system' provided Hefina with an emergency telephone. This was situated in her bedroom with a very inviting large red button on the front. She also had a mobile button which she kept on a cord around her neck, this was for when she could not reach the phone. The Lifeline was only ever used when the grandchildren couldn't resist pressing the big red button!

In 2003, Hefina's brother, John had been working on a project to have their fathers book published. 'The Ideal Miner' was brought to press. Their father, Thomas Idris Lewis was the model for the sculpture called 'The Ideal Miner' that now adorns the Big Pit Museum at Blaenafon, South Wales. The book is a story of the life of a miner, the history of coal and the terrible disasters that affected these men, families and communities. The book launch was held at the Big Pit Museum. Many of the family gathered along with TV and newspaper journalists. Some members of the family were interviewed by the Welsh channel S4C. Not long after this, his second book was published, 'Blaendulais'. This was a brief history of Seven Sisters. Copies were printed and bought for each family member who wanted one.

* * *

2003 also saw Alison and Russell's eldest son, Daniel join the Welsh Guards. After training he was deployed to Iraq and stationed there from 2004 to 2005. It was a very worrying time for everyone. However he returned safe and sound with news of an imminent wedding. In 2007 he married and on 15th February, 2008 his daughter Ffion Haf was born. She was Hefina's first great granddaughter.

During Daniel's time in the army, Hefina had the opportunity to visit Windsor Castle to witness the presentation of the new colours to the battalion. She wore a sky blue suit and a hat that would have been fitting in her mother's era. She travelled around in a wheelchair for this day and news had it that she was quite a diva, but she enjoyed nonetheless!

In December, 2005 Hefina was interviewed by Jacqueline Alkema, a Cardiff based artist originally from Kropswolde, Netherlands. She was planning an exhibition titled 'Striking Past of Women on Canvas'. This exhibition would include portraits of six Welsh women who played prominent parts during the miners' strike of 1984-85. She used oil on canvas and later wrote the life story of each woman on their faces. The exhibition was held at Muni Arts Centre in Pontypridd from Jaunary to February 2006. When Hefina saw the painting she was not best pleased, it was not something she liked at all and wasn't afraid to say so!

On 8th June, 2010 Hefina celebrated her 80th birthday. The immediate family gathered at the Abercraf Inn for a birthday bash! Dementia had unfortunately started to show itself. Although Hefina was good at hiding it, it was clear she couldn't identify people or remember things. Thankfully she enjoyed her day. This would be the last time the whole family would be together. (2010 also saw Jayne and Stuart divorce).

* * *

Alex had finished at Aberystwyth University by now and was living back at home. He rallied around as much as he could. He was a great support to Alison, helping out in any emergency. One particular event had him racing to Neath town centre. The Dulais Valley Partnership minibus would journey to Neath and back taking the villagers shopping once a week. On this particular day Hefina didn't return to the bus. They waited until they could wait no longer. Christine (a family member) was driving the minibus on this particular day, and she rang Alison to tell her that Hefina was lost in town. Alex eventually found her in Morrisons, sitting and waiting; she had lost all track of time.

By 2011, Ian, Alison and Jayne had decided it was safer for Hefina to move out of her home. By now Alison was dealing with all her mother's finances, making sure she was taking her tablets correctly and checking in on her daily. Hefina had been falling over more often both at home and when she was out. Her mind had deteriorated and she had become a liability to herself. It was decided that she would apply for a flat in Llwynon, Crynant. She had a few friends who already lived there, Edwina being one of them.

Her stay at Llwynon would not be a long one. During her time at the flat she showed increasing signs of dementia, taking walks to the shop and spending all her money on sweets and cakes. She took herself on a bus ride to Seven Sisters one day, luckily she returned this time. They tried to keep her in but it became impossible. She began to do silly and dangerous things in the flat, such as turning the microwave on with a metal saucepan inside. However, before the family could decide what to do for the best she ended up in hospital. It was August 2011. She did go home to the flat on one occasion but before long she was back. The residents of Llwynon complained of her knocking them awake in the night, but her ill health took her back to hospital where she would remain until January 2012.

On 28th March, 2011 Hefina's youngest sister, Norma, died suddenly of a heart attack. Even though Hefina attended the funeral service where her eldest sister spoke, she was not aware of the actual situation. Later that year, on 3rd October, 2011 her brother John passed away. He had been suffering with Motor Neuron disease and was living in a hospice. He died of a secondary infection. Hefina was not aware of John's passing.

This was a very difficult time for Hefina's remaining children. The decision to move Hefina into a care home did not come easily for them. Alison and Jayne visited many care homes around the valley before deciding that Ty-Mawr in Abercraf would be suitable for Hefina.

Soon, Hefina's mind had totally deteriorated, she didn't recognise the family even though she still pretended to. She didn't seem happy at Ty-Mawr but it was the best place for her at the time. She suffered a few set backs and a few infections but kept going as always.

On 18th February, 2013 Hefina's eldest sister Verona passed away in hospital. She was totally oblivious to this too. She was now the last survivor of the Lewis children.

Hefina saw her 83rd birthday in June, 2013. Her hair was white, she looked very much like her mother; she had aged and lost quite a bit of weight.

Pneumonia took a hold of Hefina on Friday 4th October, 2013. She was very unwell. Alison contacted Jayne and Ian and they decided to see how she was through the night before determining whether to travel to Wales to visit. Alison spoke to the staff at Ty-Mawr on the Saturday morning who told her that her mother seemed better. Alison visited that morning. This was to be Hefina's last day. By 3pm on 5th October, 2013 she closed her eyes and passed on peacefully, to be reunited with all her loved ones who she had lost so tragically throughout her life.

In parliament on the evening of the 9th October, Hywel Francis made a short tribute to Hefina.

> "I think, in my neighbouring constituency, of Hefina Headon, who died at the weekend – a campaigner with the Air Training Corps and Banwen Pony club and the secretary of the Neath, Dulais and Swansea Valley Miners' Support Group."

Additionally, the South Wales Evening Post wrote an article published on 15th October. The front page read:

> "HEART OF THE VALLEY. As Wales commemorates the countys worst mining disaster, tributes paid to community stalwart who supported the strike."

The story itself read:

> "Heart of the valley miners' strike campaigner dies.
>
> Tributes have been paid to a Dulais Valley woman who organised community help during the miners' strike of the 1980s.
>
> Hefina Headon, who set up support during the year-long strike of 1984-85, died last week after a long illness. She has been described as the heart of the valley by those who knew her.
>
> And the campaigner has also been hailed by Neath MP Peter Hain for being the "heart of our valleys". Her funeral will be held at Llwydcoed Crematorium this Thursday. In tribute Mr Hain said: "Like me, many local people were very sad to learn of Hefina's death after a serious illness. Her service to the community and the Labour Party was fantastic and many were in debt to her for her hard work

and care for others. As a Labour stalwart, Hefina served as Treasurer for the Seven Sisters Branch and was an active ward member. She also showed me tremendous personal support for which I will forever be grateful. I will always remember with great fondness Hefina holding the Neath, Dulais and Swansea Valley Women's Support Group banner from the 1984 to 1985 Miners' Strike outside Parliament when I was first introduced as Neath's MP. I know of the tireless activity she undertook during the strike to support the miners and their families who were then suffering so badly. The courage and determination she showed with many other local women was an inspiration at a terrible time. For this vital contribution and all her other selfless community work, her name will stand proud forever. She was a heart of our Welsh Valley communities, such a colourful, outgoing character that brought so much bubbly happiness to everyone with whom she came into contact."

Councillor Steve Hunt, Neath Port Talbot Council ward member for Seven Sisters, described Hefina as a second mum to him. "I grew up with her and her family, she lived in Cae Mawr which was around the corner from me," he said "I had the utmost respect for her growing up, she was quite stern and made sure she put me on the right track. She was a strong woman and she was absolutely brilliant. I know she'd had some illnesses for a while. I thought the world of her, she will be missed by many, many people, she was a stalwart of the village, a real character, honest to God."

He said he'd only become aware of Hefina's passing yesterday and added that he had many memories of being around her as a child".

The cremation was held at Llwydcoed Crematorium on Thursday 17th October, 2013. The officiating minister was Gareth Hopkin, a former teacher at Ystalyfera secondary Welsh school which Ian, Alison and Jayne all attended.

Peter Lloyd, ward member of Seven Sisters Labour Party read out a letter sent by Peter Hain MP. It was addressed to Alison for the whole family and said similar words as printed in the Evening Post article.

The service sang 'Morning Has Broken' and 'Calon Lan'. The prayer was 'Gweddi Yr Arglwydd' (The Lord's Prayer in Welsh).

Ein Tad, yr hwn wyt yn y nefoedd
Sancteiddier dy enw;
Deled dy deyrnas;
Gwneler dy ewyllys;
Megis yn y nef, felly ar y ddaear hefyd.
Dyro I ni heddiw ein bara beunyddiol.
Fel y maddeuwn ninnau I'n dyledwyr.
Ac nac arwain ni I brofedigaeth;
Eithr gwared ni rhad drwg.
Canys eiddot ti yw'r deyrnas,
A'r gallu, a'r gogoniant,
Yn oes oesoedd.

AMEN

CHAPTER 9

Hefina's Legacy

For most people, the legacy of their life lives on in their families, in memories and photographs. Stories are carried through generations until they become a distant memory lost in history. The same cannot be said for Hefina. The film 'Pride' has embedded a part of her in the lives of millions of people and the archives of British film. Her stalwart nature and the part she so significantly played in the 1984-85 miners' strike is her main legacy.

Louise Carolin of DIVA magazine interviewed Stephen Beresford, Mike Jackson, Nicola Field and Jayne Headon-Meldrum prior to the film release (see article on page 140-141).

The film was released in September, 2014. The premiere was held in Camden, London. Tickets were obtained from Pathé and the family attended: Alison, Ian, Jackie, Christopher, Mathew, Sean, Jayne and her partner Emily.

Before the film began, the actors entered the cinema from the rear doors. Speeches were made by Matthew Warchus and Stephen Beresford, who then asked all those involved in the strike to stand. The actors and audience could see the real people behind the film. There was a lengthy round of applause. At the end of the film, emotions ran high and tears were in abundance. The film received a standing ovation and an enormous round of applause.

Afterwards, the family met Imelda Staunton, the actress who played Hefina in the film. Jayne asked her if she was proud of the film. She replied "If I didn't work again, I will be proud to say I played such a strong character", she said she felt as though Hefina's life had ended and was now passing the gauntlet on. She made it her mission to play the part to the best of her ability and she did it so well.

One of Britain's best character actresses, Imelda Staunton, plays committee stalwart Hefina. "Hefina passed away and I felt she was saying 'OK, I've done my bit, now you carry on.' I wasn't saddened by it as, my goodness she did her part. But of course because the characters are real you feel a huge responsibility," says Staunton. "Stephen's screenplay was a beautifully written story, with a lot of laughing and crying, and it took me back to those times that were so frustrating. It looks at the subject with humour, heart, great poignancy and reality. This manages to make it a story based on mostly real characters that is a very watchable account of a very bad time in a lot of people's lives. But if you can introduce humour into things you can also take them very seriously and this film does that. Quite a few issues are addressed in this film, but you wouldn't know it, which is what I love about it. You're laughing and laughing and then you suddenly think, 'I can't believe people really thought like that.' It pulls you in with humour and then the humour pulls you up short. There's nothing better. And it changed the Welsh village forever. It enriched their lives."

Courtesy of Pathé production notes

As a result of the film, both the LGSM (Lesbians and Gays Support the Miners) and the Neath, Dulais and Swansea Valley Miners' Support groups re-established themselves. The LGSM support causes they feel they can make a difference to. The Welsh support group was initially set up to organise and celebrate the 30th Glorious Twelfth event. This was held at the Onllwyn Welfare (The Palace of Culture) on 14th March, 2015.

Jayne and Alison presented Hefina's banner to the Miners Library to keep in their archives as part of the strike-rich history. It was an extremely successful evening. Many friends old and new came together to celebrate. Money raised was given in cheque format and presented to the LGSM for the Mark Ashton Red Ribbon Fund (Part of the Terrence Higgins Trust) for the sum of £4,000. These groups will continue to fight and support worthy causes.

Hywel Francis MP re-launched his book and dedicated it to Hefina and Mark Ashton. The book is titled "History On Our Side – Wales &

the 1984-85 Miners' Strike".

On 2nd June, 2015 Christina Rees MP for Neath included Hefina in her Maiden Speech:

"In March, there was the 30th anniversary of the formation of the miners' support group that was set up by Hefina Headon and others. The anniversary was celebrated in the Onllwyn Miners Welfare Club, which is otherwise known as the palace of culture. Bronwen Lewis sang "Bread and Roses", as she did in the film "Pride". The words of the song and Bronwen's beautiful voice reduced us all to tears.

"Pride" was filmed in Banwen, the home of the DOVE Workshop, which was set up by Hefina, Councillor Moira Lewis and Mair Francis at the end of the miners' strike. DOVE retrained women to work because the men had lost their jobs, but later it opened its doors to men as well."

Along with this biography, these tributes will add to the legacy of a formidable stalwart whose life was dedicated to the Labour Party and the community.

May her memory live on in all of us.

SECTION 2

LIFE
IN
PHOTOGRAPHS

The following collection of photographs correspond with each chapter of the biography.

CHAPTER 1   The Early Years

The Phillips family 1918
Back L-R Catherine, William, Papa (John) Thomas, Eva
Front L-R Bryn, Lillian, Baby Ronald, Louisa (Nana), Richard

Catherine (Katie) and Thomas Idris 1932
Hefina's mother and father

Hefina aged 4 years - 1934

Hefina aged 3 years - 1933

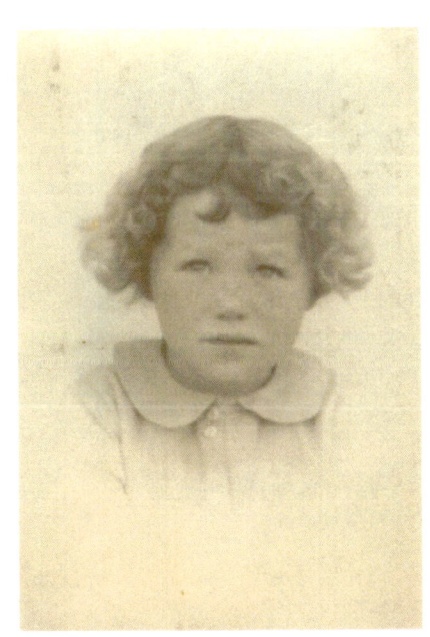

Hefina aged 4 years - 1934

Hefina aged 5 years - 1935

1936 - The Lewis Children
John, Hefina, Verona and Norma (baby)
at Tan-y-Coed Bungalow

1936
A family outing to the beach
Known faces -
Katie, Tommy, Lil, Eva, Iris,
Moira Davies, John, Hefina
(front right),
Verona with Norma

Hefina's Siblings

Verona -
Hefina's older sister

John -
Hefina's older brother

Norma -
Hefina's younger sister

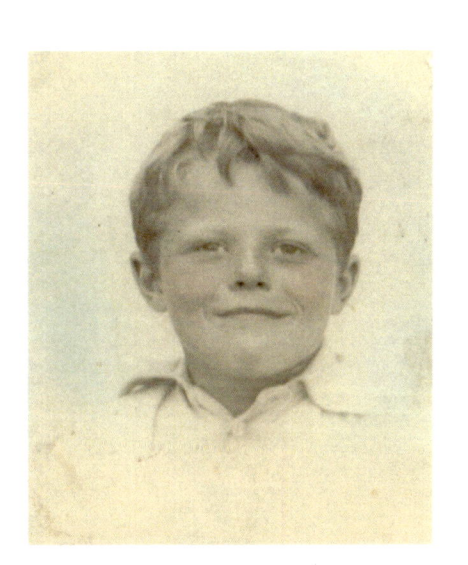

School Photo 1935 - Hefina middle row 4th from right John Headon back row 5th from left

1934
Verona (back)
Moira Davies (left)
John (centre)
Hefina (right)

Hefina aged 15 years -
1945
with her sister Norma

CHAPTER 2 Journey Into Adulthood

Hefina and Johnny Smith's wedding July 1947

Wedding: Lewis—Smith. — The wedding was solemnized at Zoar Chapel on Tuesday of last week between Miss Hefina Lewis, daughter of Mr. and Mrs. T. I. Lewis, Tan y Coed, Seven Sisters, and Mr. David John Smith, son of Mr. and Mrs. James Charles Smith, 13, Heol y Marchog, Banwen. The Rev. Howel William officiated and the organist was Mrs. M. Price.

Given away by her father, the bride was attired in a gown of ivory chiffon velvet, with full length veil held in place by a wreath of orange blossoms. She carried a bouquet of saffron pink rosebuds. The matrons of honour, Mrs. Verona Bamford and Mrs. Iris Morgan, wore gowns of pink and turquoise figured taffeta, respectively, with feathered headdresses, and carried bouquets of sweet peas. The bride was presented with a silver horseshoe by her cousin, Kerry Dorgan. Mr. William Williams was the best man and Mr. John Lewis the groomsman. Over 40 guests attended the reception, which was held at the Waverley Hotel, Neath, where numerous telegrams were read. The groom's gift to the bride was a pearl necklace; the bride's gift to the groom was a signet ring, while the bridesmaids received pearl earings surmounted with diamonds. The honeymoon was spent at Carmarthen, the bride travelling in an off-white coat with brown accessories. The bride was on the staff of the Seven Sisters Post Office, while the bridegroom has been an active member of the Onllwyn Y.M.C.A. for many years.

Newspaper article
Lewis & Smith
wedding
1947

Johnny Smith 1935

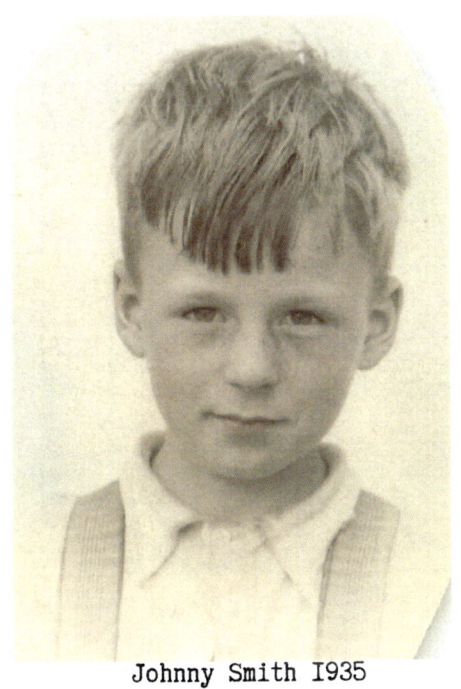

Rachel Hannah & James Smith

Norma - Chaperone with Hefina and Johnny

David, March 1950

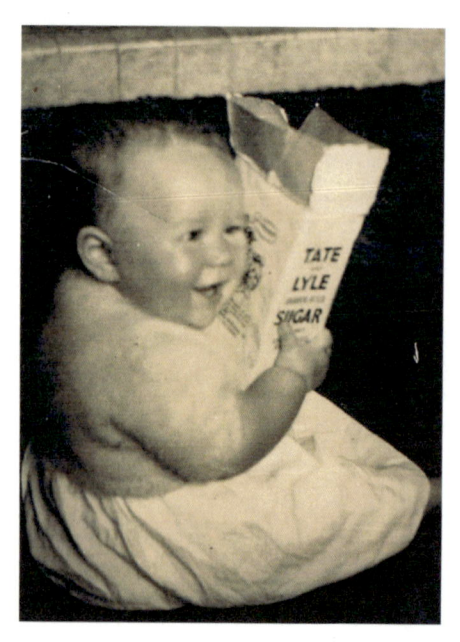

Jennifer 1952

Johnny, Hefina & David, Tripoli

80

Jennifer & David 1953

Jennifer

The Decree Absolute

[Certificate of making Decree Nisi Absolute (Divorce).]

S 19 53 , (D) No. 67

In the High Court of Justice.

PROBATE, DIVORCE AND ADMIRALTY DIVISION
(DIVORCE).

DISTRICT REGISTRY.

Between

Nefina Smith   *Petitioner*

and

David John Smith   *Respondent*

and   *Co-Respondent*

Referring to the decree made in this Cause on the 15 day of MAY 1953, whereby it was decreed that the Marriage had and solemnized on the 8th day of July 19 47 , at Zoar Congregational Chapel, Seven Sisters in the District of Neath in the County of Glamorgan

between

Nefina Smith (then Lewis) Spinster the Petitioner

and

David John Smith

the Respondent

be dissolved by reason that since the celebration thereof the said Respondent had been guilty of adultery

unless sufficient cause be shown to the Court within six weeks from the making thereof why the said Decree should not be made absolute, and no such cause having been shown, it is hereby certified that the said Decree was on the 30 day of JUNE 1953 19 , made final and absolute and that the said Marriage was thereby dissolved.

Dated the 30 day of JUNE 19 1953

(List No. 38).

M52393/D84.45m.8/52.LC.817.(4908)

82

CHAPTER 3 The Challenging Era

Daniel & Hilda Mary Headon
John's mother & father

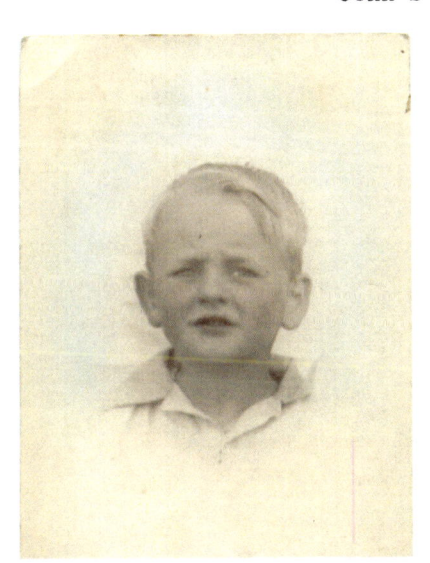

Reginald John Headon
Aged 5 & 7 years

Joan, John & Lillian 1946

Reginald John Headon
Approx 1936/7 aged 7

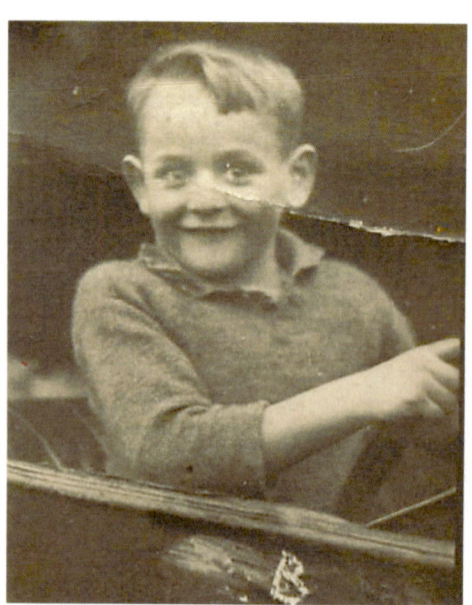

Reginald John Headon
Age 16 years

John & Hefina at the dances in
Blackpool, September 1956

Reginald John Headon
Age 18 years

Mid 50s, John & Hefina out with friends John & Mary & Hefina's
sister Norma & her husband, Dennis Newton (then courting)

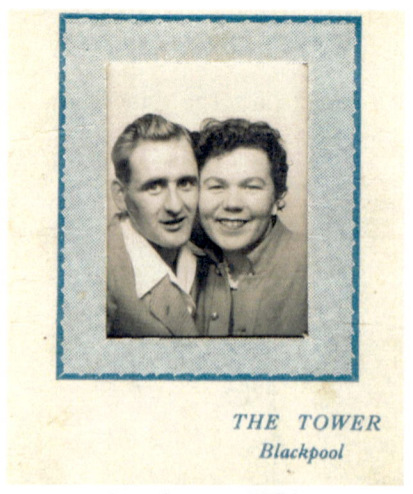

Blackpool 1956

Another night at the dances
1956

Hefina
Protecting herself from the sun
1955

Hefina & friend Eira (later to become Alison's mother in law)
1954

Good times with her friend Peggy 1950s
Peggy's husband Lynn was the best man at John & Hefina's wedding.

Sibling Weddings

Norma & Dennis Newton
Christine, Jennifer & Tessa
as flower girls

Verona & Tommy Bamford

John & Mary Lewis

John & Hefina's wedding
March 1958

David & Jennifer

1957

1958

1959

David, Jennifer & Martyn
1958

90

1954

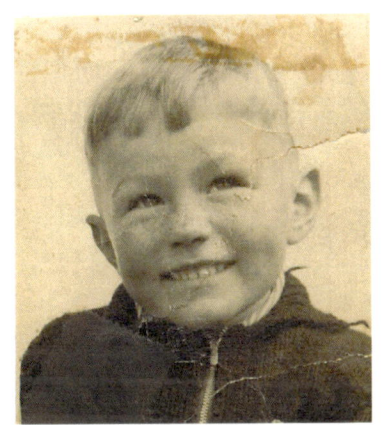

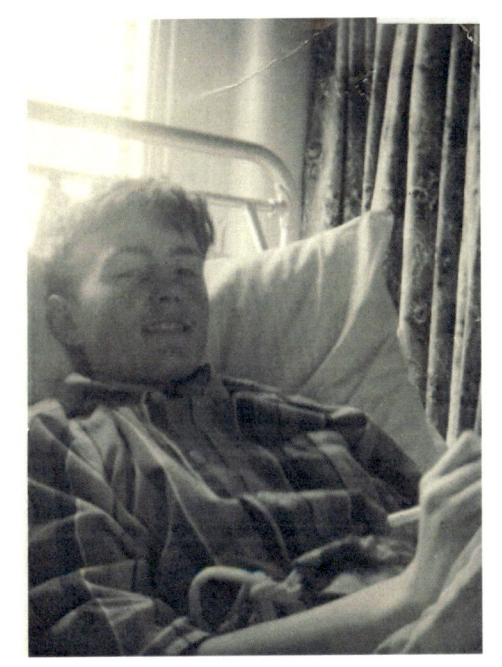

1962 in hospital

1961
Martyn front David 3rd row right

91

Ian 1961

Ian 1962

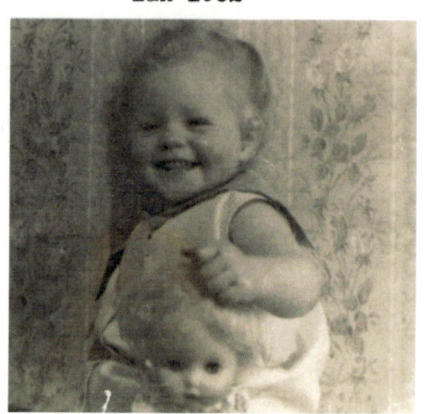

Alison 1962

Alison 1963

Hefina with Ian & Alison
1962

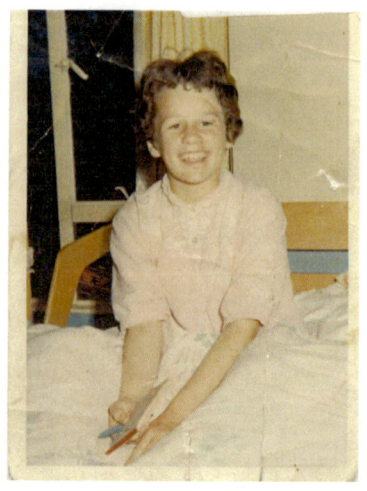

Jennifer after accident 1963

Visiting Jennifer in Cardiff 1967
Jennifer, Hefina, John, Jennifer's friend, Alison & Ian

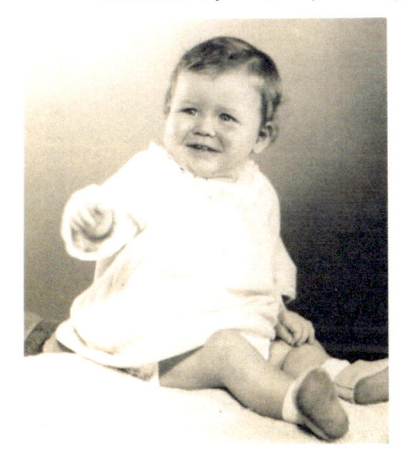

Jayne 1968

Jennifer & Jayne at Barnado's 1968

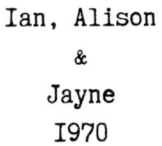

Ian, Alison & Jayne 1970

CHAPTER 4 Moving Forward

The Onllwyn Welfare Miners Club

The Onllwyn Post Office

The Onllwyn Inn

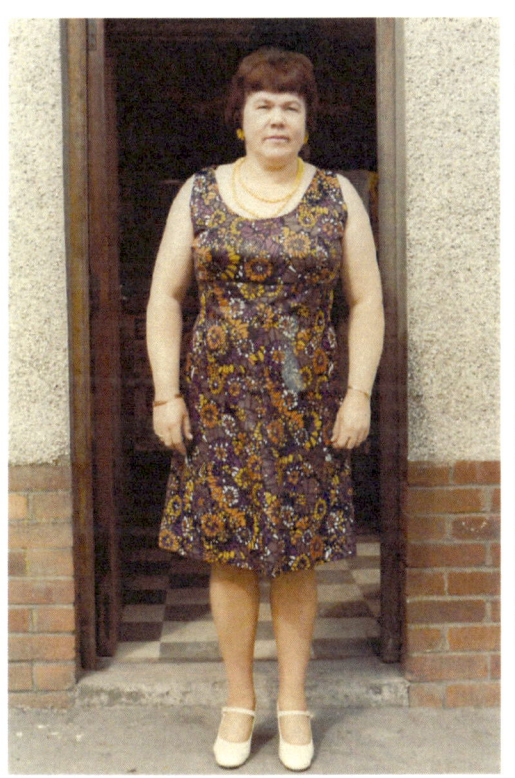

Hefina at the back door of the Onllwyn Post Office 1975

Hefina, Ian, Jayne (Mick the dog) holding the promotion boxes of Wrigley's Spearmint gum

At the back of the Onllwyn Post Office, Jayne, Jennifer, Alison & Ian 1975/6

The Banwen Carnival Club
Hefina dressed up as:

Above: Chelsea Pensioners 1977

Below: Fairy 1973

Right: Nora Battie from Last of the Summer Wine 1976

YMCA Group
1974
Caldicot
Castle
Medieval
Night

Tara club night with the Post Office groups and Kay's fruit and veg shop 1974

A wedding in Bristol with the Pony Club 1974
L>R back - Mary Lewis, Hefina.
L>R Middle - Beattie Kemeys, Shirley Tancock, Gwyneth Morgan, Mrs T Lewis, Enid Jones, Madge Henton.
L>R front - Betty Miller, Glenys Jones, Marian Thomas, Jenny Parfitt & Jean Jones

Aberavon
day out
1975

Tenby Holiday
with Pony Club
friends 1977

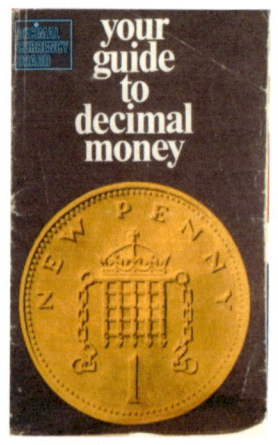

Prepared by the Decimal Currency Board and the Central Office of
Information 1972

On Board HMS
Fife, family day
visiting Ian
1978

4 Generations
Jennifer
Hefina
Katie
Jayne
August 1978

1973-75 Easter Bonnet competition YMCA Pinafore Club.

1973-75 Pony Club event

Pony Club presenting a TV to Cimla Hospital 1974
L>R Hospital staff Beattie Kemeys, Jean Jones, Hefina, Matron, Ivor Jones, Jenny Parfitt, hospital staff member.

CHAPTER 5 Community Spirit

Above & right the girls from the Arthritis fundraisng Committee.

Ist July I983 The Centenary celebration at the Playscheme. Blaendulais School I883 - I983

Collecting money for the Playscheme dressed up as a fairy.

101

Enjoying the sun 1980

Another chance to dress up. - Note: those are fake breasts!

Auntie Lil, Katie, Jennifer & Hefina

With her Mam at the Tara Club 1983

Another chance to be a fairy.

Right: Being silly!

Below: 'The pyjamas' Blackpool 1988

Middle right: She was always encouraging John to dress as a woman

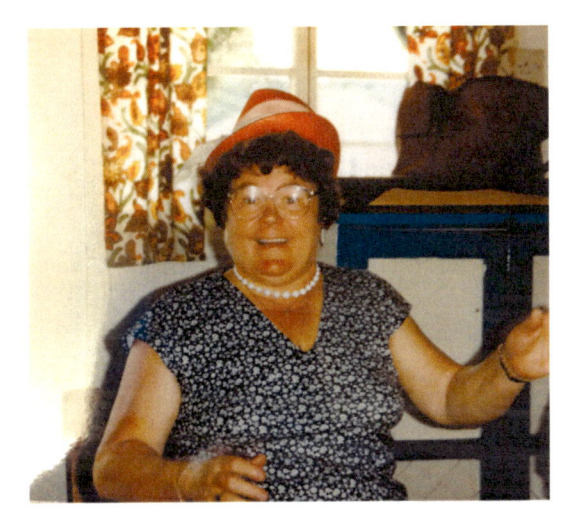

Typical faces of two people who were still very much in love

1983 - Jayne & Hefina at the Tara Club.

Dulwich Park - London on a visit to see Jennifer 1980

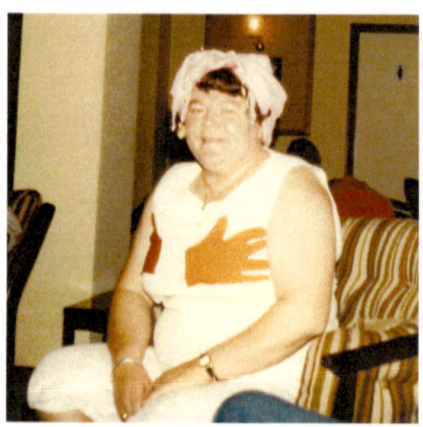

Hefina - dressing up in 'the pyjamas'

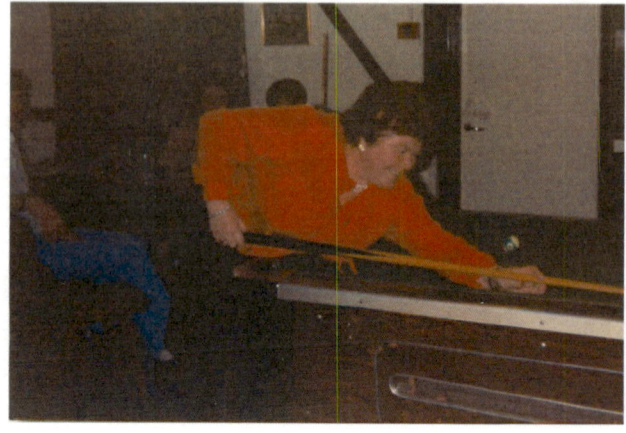

A smart attempt to play Pool!

Jayne, Alison & Jennifer 1983 The Castle, Trecastle. Alison's 21st birthday

Above: Ian & Jackie 1982
Left: Ian on HMS Fife 1979

105

29th August 1981
Alison marries Russell Williams

16th November 1983
Jennifer marries Steven Vigue

Hefina's son Ian's wedding
Summer 1984
Below: family picture which includes the new addition -
Daniel Williams

CHAPTER 6 Significant Differences

13th November 1984
'My Claim to Fame' on the platform at the Afon Lido - standing ovation in front of 6500 people. Arthur Scargill, President of NUM, Peter Heathfield, Mick McGahey, Terry Thomas & others on the stage.
Image courtesy of The South Wales Evening Post

Left:
Hay BBQ
July 1985
Hefina with 'the van'

Below:
Seven Sisters Rec 1985 with
Christine Powell and 'the van'

Hefina & her long time
friend the mischievous
Edwina Roberts enjoing
an ice cream in
Bournemouth 1985

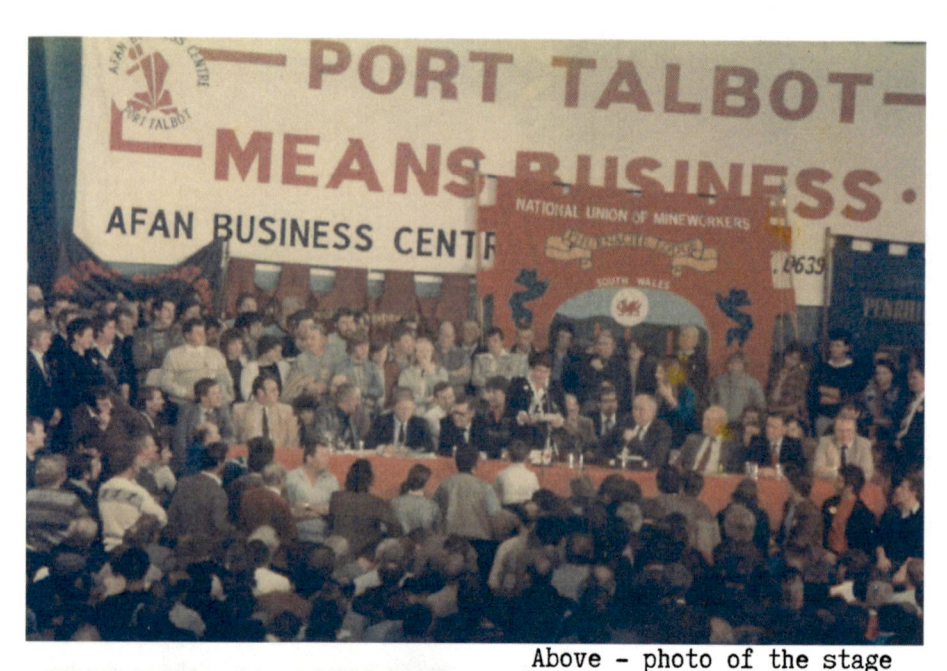

Above - photo of the stage

Arthur Scargill with Hefina
Image Courtesy of Media Wales,
formerly - the Western Mail &
Echo Ltd

Poster of the event

110

19th May 1984 - Rally

Support group meeting Onllwyn Welfare

A car full of donated bread and milk and a corridor full of donated food for the parcels

A Christmas card designed and printed by The Rhymni Valley Miners' Support Group - bought by Hefina for her Sister Verona - Christmas 1984

Above: Hefina, John & Jayne at the Onllwyn Welfare 1984
Below: Dancing 1985

Article regarding turkeys for every miner's family at Christmas, South Wales Evening Post 30/11/84

112

Coelbren Club
2 March 1985
Sian, Karen,
Christine &
Hefina

Flying Pickets
evening 1985
Stuart Powell
with Hefina from
the support
group with David
Brett &
Gareth Williams
of the Flying
Pickets

Left: Hefina with
Arthur Scargil

Below: 6th April 1985 Ystrad
Welfare

LGSM
visiting
The Onllwyn
Welfare Hall
1984

Photos of and by LGSM - courtesy of.
Ray, Reggie, Gethin, Mike, Mark

Trip to London
with LGSM
"Maggie for the
Tower!"

The 'van' in colour

The 'van' with LGSM members

Lobbying the miners at Crynant who were dicussing the return to work call. 26 February, 1985

Photos by Imogen Young

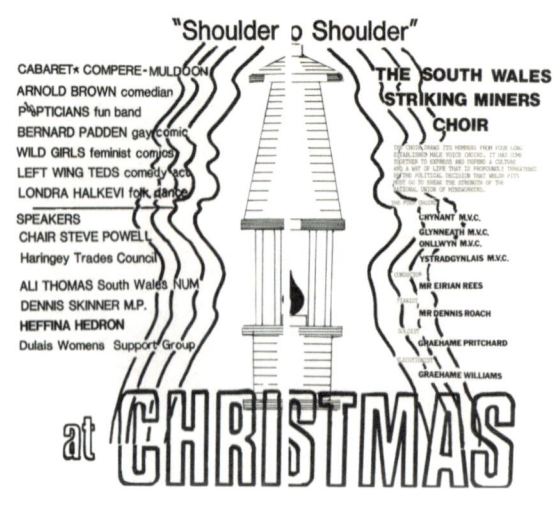

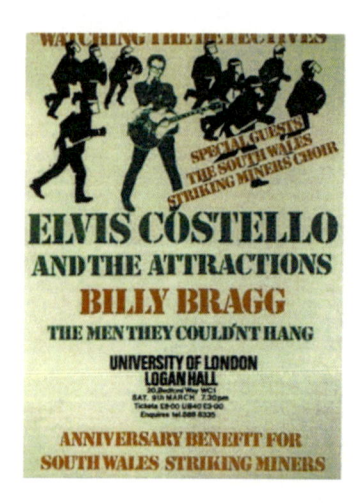

Posters & Programmes of support events 1984-85

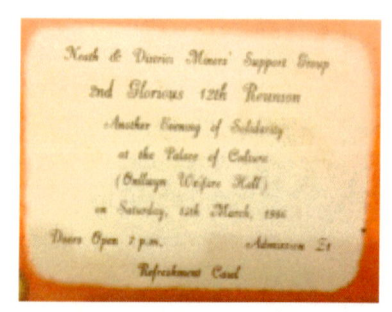

Courtesy of Kevin Franklin

Original ticket to the 1st Glorious Twelfth

116

The banner & the badge

The famous notes left for each other at home - usually instructions and messages

Copy of the handwritten poem by Hefina

Turn Liver
& Chops
over.

Take Liver out,
first chop on its
own to be cooked
the most.

Auntie Rona has got flu.
She won't be down this weekend.

They Tried To Starve us Out,
    You were there
We Needed Food Donations
    You were there
We Needed Strength on Demonstrations,
    You were there
When we Needed Help To Picket
    You were there
Whatever Help or Task, We only had to ask
We need not have worried
    You were there.
The Papers Tried To Tell us
    You weren't there
Maggie Tried To Tell us, You weren't there,
Oh! Where could they be looking
What did they think they were cooking
You certainly showed them You were there,
Word's cant express our thanks
    For being there
We will always remember
    Your being there
And if ever you need us
    You only have to call
As we can Guarantee We'll be there
        Diolch - Donation

117

NGA Men visit Singing - Hefina, Ann, Gwyneth and Chris John to the left of the picture

Scarlett Harletts visit

Member of the SH, Hefina, Pat Davies, Winnie Barrel, Jean Rees & Susan Lewis 27/0I/85

The first celebration of the Glorious I2th held at the Onllwyn Welfare 'Palace of Culture'. March I985

CHAPTER 7 Rolling Along

At one of the Community Centre disco nights

Hefina, Verona, Ronald Lewis & Janice (cousins)

Hefina with her mother Katie Lewis, her Auntie Lil Phillips & Jayne at Bishop Meadows January 1986

Jayne's 18th birthday family gathering

119

The newspaper article on
Paul Robeson Jnr's visit in
March 1989
Courtesy of:
The Western Mail

Above: Paul Robeson Jnr
Edwina & Hefina
1986
Below: The funeral service
of Paul Robeson Snr
presented to Hefina October
1986

*To Hefina Headley
with warm regards
Paul Robeson, Jr.
Oct 23,
1986*

APRIL 9TH, 1898 — JANUARY 23RD, 1976

FUNERAL SERVICE FOR PAUL ROBESON

Tuesday, January 27th, 1976 - 8 p.m.

MOTHER A.M.E. ZION CHURCH
New York, New York

Sons of famous fathers further human rights

HUMAN RIGHTS speaker Paul Robeson (left) meets with Dr Howell Francis.

TWO SONS of famous fathers got together in Swansea yesterday to help further the cause of human rights.

Writer Paul Robeson — whose actor father of the same name became a firm favourite with South Wales miners when he made a film in the Principality in the 1940s — was at the city's university college to deliver a memorial lecture.

He was met by the head of the college's adult education department, Dr Howell Francis, the son of former miners' leader Mr Dai Francis.

A college spokesman said yesterday, "It was quite fitting to have two sons of famous fathers together and there is also a strong mining connection between them. They had plenty to talk about."

Last night at the college, Mr Robeson delivered the Eileen Illtyd David Memorial Lecture on the theme of human rights.

The lecture is held annually in memory of the wife of former college lecturer, the late Dr Illtyd David.

Following the death of Dr David himself, colleagues collected money to ensure that the tradition of human rights lectures continued at Swansea.

Past lecture speakers have included Bruce Kent, Tariq Ali, Lord Scarman, Lord Elwyn Jones and Lord Jenkins.

Mr Robeson fitted the college's invitation to speak into his present lecture tour of Britain. He has already spoken at universities in Durham and Manchester.

As a child, he followed his father around the world as the popular man pursued his career as a singer and actor.

As a result, son Paul lived in England, Europe and the Soviet Union, and is now a fluent Russian speaker.

From 1942-45 he was his father's personal representative and acted for him on a number of occasions when he was refused entry into recording studios and theatres.

He looked after his father until his death in 1976, and now regularly contributes to international magazines and writes books.

At the weekend, the American writer and journalist was Guest of Honour at Onllwyn Miners' Welfare Hall near Neath.

Officials at the hall held a special evening to raise money for the Armenian Earthquake Appeal and to raise cash for the Nicaraguan Hurricane Relief Appeal.

John and their dog
Boomer

Jayne -
Womens'
Royal
Army
Corps
July
1986

Above - Hefina & John 1988
Courtesy of
Reggie Blennerhassett

Below - Dusseldorf, Germany
1988

Lil Phillips embroidering at
92 years old

Jayne's wedding 1989

40th Wedding Anniversary and a broken ankle 1990

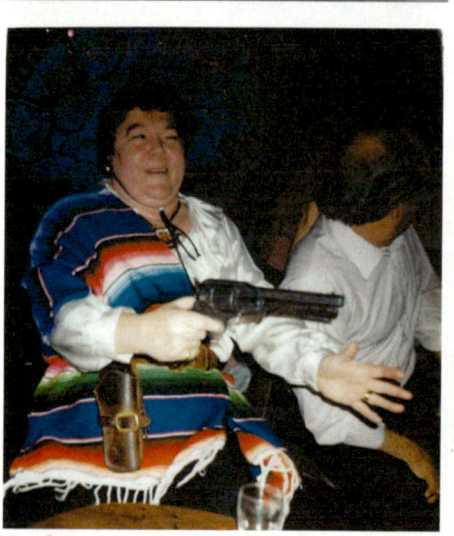

Cowboy night - Onllwyn Welfare raising funds for the Eisteddfod

Top: Peter Hain - 'Save our Bank' with Elaine Powell
Middle: Peter Hain at Parliament
Bottom: The Labour Party with Peter Hain, Seven Sisters ward

Jacuzzi opening
Christine, Edwina & Hefina

Playing bowls in Ystrad

David Morris Euro MP Strazburg July 1992

Partners in crime - Hefina & Edwina

Family picture outside the house in Cae Mawr
Back: Ian, Jackie, Hefina, Russell, Stuart
Front: Alex, John, Christopher, Daniel, Jayne
Alison taking the photo, September 1990

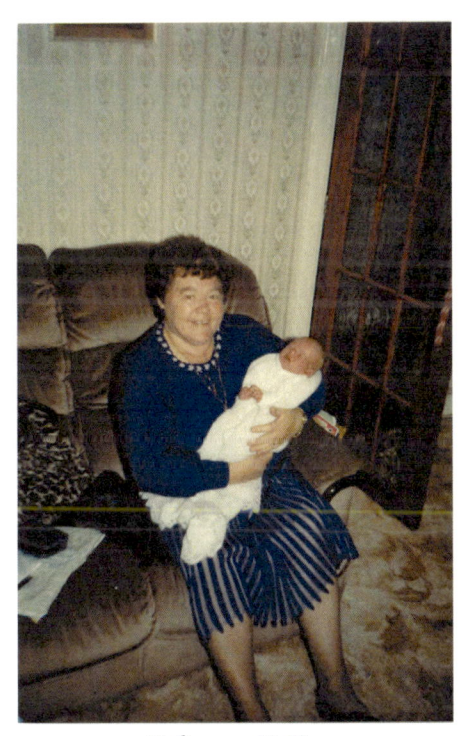

Hefina & Mathew

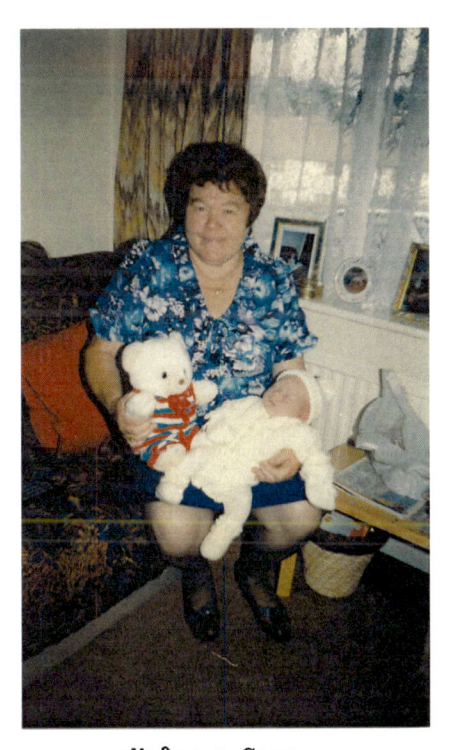

Hefina & Sean

125

Ron of NGA 27/II/90
Onllwyn Welfare

On the steam train at
Blaenant Colliery

Hefina & her sister Verona at the
Jubilee Rooms, Houses of Parliament
20th June 1994

More fun dressing up

Hefina, Jayne, Alison &
Sean, SS carnival

10th Anniversary of the Women's Bowls team
June 1996

Verona - Mayoress
1997

Verona - Mayoress
Mary & John Lewis
Tessa & Verona
Auntie Lil Phillips
Hefina & Norma

Banwen rugby winning Brewers cup
Post House hotel, Cardiff Barbara O'Brian, Ian & Hefina

Typical home life,
Hefina was a hoarder!

Typical night out enjoing together

All 8 Grandsons
L>R
Owen, Alex, Ashley
Sean holding Gregg
sitting on
Christopher
Mathew & Daniel
1998

Brother and
sisters:
Norma
John
Hefina
Verona
at Sara's
Wedding
1998

Christmas dinner
together
Quite a rarity!

129

CHAPTER 8 A Grand Finale

Church Garden Party
2005

Soar
Congregation
30/06/06

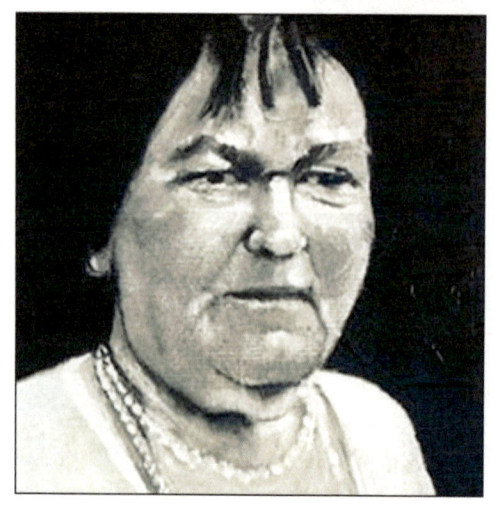

This is a drawing created by
Jacqeline Alkema
who created a series of 6
women titled
"Women with a Past"
The initial context is the
Miners' Strike of 1984/85,
the image offers a thrilling
fusion of words made flesh.
Hefina did not like this
drawing at all!
2006

'The Ideal Miner' book launch
The statue - above
Hefina with Phillip Lewis

Below, Hefina & her siblings
Verona, John & Norma with the book

Windsor Castle with Daniel 2007

Daniel's wedding 2007

Jayne, Hefina, Ian & Alison

The grandsons:

Back: Christopher, Alex, Daniel, Mathew, Sean
Front: Owen, Hefina, Gregg & Ashley

Ian's family:
Christopher
Jackie
Ian
Mathew
&
Ashley
2007

Alison's family:
Alex
Russell
Alison
&
Daniel

2002

Jayne's family:
Gregg
Jayne
Owen
&
Sean

2010

Mathew & Ashley Headon

Gregg, Sean & Owen Meldrum

Ffion Haf

Left: Newborn Feb 2008
below:
6 months old
Bottom left:
I year old

Christmas celebrations at Trem-y-Glyn

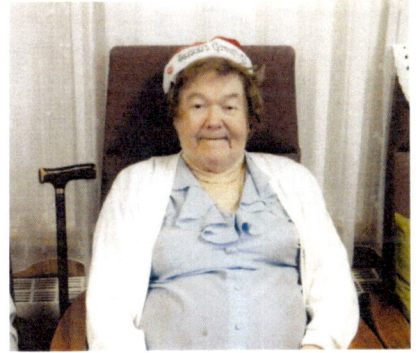

Janice, Beryl, Audrey and Anne. At Beryl's Anniversary 2009

Labour Party Seven Sisters Ward

From the book 'Up The DOVE'
written by & courtesy of Mair Francis

Official opening of the 'extension on the extension', with Joy Howells, Lesley Smith, Julie Bibby, Hefina Headon and Mair Francis, January 2004. (Photo by DOVE Workshop)

Hefina's 80th
Birthday

Hefina & Norma

Norma
John
Verona
&
Hefina
at John's 80th Birthday

The last photo
taken of Hefina on her
83rd birthday
8th June 2013
with Jayne
Sean, Owen,
Gregg & Jayne's
campervan,
Penelope!

'Heart of valley' miners' strike campaigner dies

By Rachel Moses-Lloyd

TRIBUTES have been paid to a Dulais Valley woman who organised community help during the miners' strike of the 1980s.

Hefina Headon, who set up support during the year-long strike of 1984 to 85, died last week after a long illness.

She has been described as the heart of the valley by those who knew her.

And the campaigner has also been hailed by Neath MP Peter Hain for being the "heart of our valleys".

Her funeral will be held at Llwydcoed Crematorium this Thursday.

In a tribute Mr Hain said: "Like me, many local people were very sad to learn of Hefina's death after a serious illness.

"Her service to the community and the Labour Party was fantastic and many were in debt to her for her hard work and care for others.

"As a Labour stalwart, Hefina served as Treasurer of the Seven Sisters Branch and was an active ward member.

"She also showed me tremendous personal support for which I will forever be grateful.

"I will always remember with great fondness Hefina holding the Neath, Dulais and Swansea Valley Women's Support Group banner from the 1984 to 1985 Miners' Strike outside Parliament when I was first introduced as Neath's MP.

"I know of the tireless activity she undertook during the strike to support the miners and their families who were then suffering so badly.

"The courage and determination she showed with many other local women was an inspiration at a terrible time.

"For this vital contribution and all her other selfless community work, her name will stand proud forever.

"She was a heart of our Welsh Valley communities, such a colourful, outgoing character that brought so much bubbly happiness to everyone with whom she came into contact."

Councillor Steve Hunt, Neath Port Talbot Council ward member for Seven Sisters, described Hefina as a second mum to him.

"I grew up with her and her family, she lived in Cae Mawr which was around the corner from me," he said.

"I had the utmost respect for her growing up, she was quite stern and made sure she put me on the right track.

"She was a strong woman and she was absolutely brilliant.

"I know she'd had some illnesses for a while.

"I though the world of her, she will be missed by many, many people, she was a stalwart of the village, a real character, honest to God."

He said he'd only become aware of Hefina's passing yesterday, and added that he had many memories of being around her as a child.

The funeral will be at Llwydcoed Crematorium on Thursday October 17 at noon.

Pay your tribute
Did you know Hefina? Pay your tribute to her online
southwales-eveningpost.co.uk

COMMUNITY CHAMPION Hefina Headon and (below, right) with Neil Kinnock and Neath MP Peter Hain during Miners' Strike.

Courtesy of the South Wales Evening Post
2013

CHAPTER 9   Hefina's Legacy

The Premiere
of 'Pride'

September 2013

With Imelda Staunton

Above:
Alison, Imelda, Jayne & Ian

Right:
Mathew, Sean, Imelda & Christopher

On the stage for the Premiere - the original LGSM and NDSV Miners Support Group. Photograph - Courtesy of Dave Hogan Pathé

DIVA Magazine with Stephen Beresford, Mike Jackson, Jayne Headon (Author) & Nicola Field
Reproduced with permission of DIVA Magazine

EVERYBODY OUT!

PRIDE IS THE DON'T-MISS FILM OF THE YEAR, TELLING AN INSPIRING TALE OF SOLIDARITY WITH WARMTH, WIT AND A LOAD OF LAUGHS. LOUISE CAROLIN TALKS TO THE REAL PEOPLE WHOSE STORIES INFORM THE AWARD-WINNING MOVIE

The gay movie of the year is set to shatter assumptions and get audiences weeping with laughter when it comes to the big screen this month (see our review, p29). Its subject: a little-known but inspiring episode in British Labour history. Written by Stephen Beresford and directed by Matthew Warchus, Pride tells the story of the lesbians and gay men who united in support of mining communities during the Miners' Strike of 1984-5.

"I was 22 when I first heard about it," says Beresford, "and I remember thinking at the time, that's the most incredible story, but I didn't actually believe it, if I'm honest."

The alliance between urban, gay activists and tight-knit, rural, working class communities may sound unlikely but looking back to the 1980s, when both groups were suffering vicious attacks under Margaret Thatcher's Tory government, it all makes sense, says Mike Jackson, a founding member of the group Lesbians and Gays Support the Miners (LGSM).

> "I THOUGHT, THAT'S THE MOST INCREDIBLE STORY, BUT I DIDN'T BELIEVE IT"

In 1984 the government declared its intention to close 20 British coal mines, provoking the National Union of Mineworkers (NUM) to call a strike. Deeming the strike illegal, the government sequestered the union's funds, leaving strikers without access to financial support. New tactics were brought in preventing the families of the "illegal" strikers from claiming benefits. By winter, striking communities were on starvation rations, harassed by police at picket lines and baited by the right-wing papers. But support groups sprang up around the country and even abroad, twinning with mining villages to deliver food, money and clothes. Pop acts including the Style Council, Bronski Beat, Elvis Costello and Billy Bragg performed benefit gigs.

"One of the reasons so many lesbians and gay men supported the miners is because there were parallels," notes Jackson. "Gay men were suffering entrapment by the police. There was routine raiding of pubs and clubs for absolutely no reason. There was a raid on Gay's The Word bookshop by Customs and Excise, supposedly to confiscate obscene material – you're talking about classic writers like Christopher Isherwood here. It was legal for people to be sacked simply because they were homosexual. Women were refused [custody of their own children] because they were lesbians."

Nevertheless, Jackson found the gay community's support for the miners astonishing: the first time he and co-founder Mark Ashton rattled their buckets, at Gay Pride 1984, they raised over £200, quite a sum for the time. Inspired by this success, Jackson and Ashton formed LGSM, the London branch of which twinned with the South Wales mining villages

"THEY WERE THE MOST FABULOUS BUNCH"

Jayne Headon-Muldrum was 16 when LGSM came to Dulais in 1984 to support the striking community. Her late mother, Hefina, is portrayed in the film by Imelda Staunton. Jayne came out as a lesbian two years ago, aged 44.

What I remember about the pride is everybody was so busy, so social. I loved the stuff my mum did and I went along to all her meetings.

Everybody was so loving, so welcoming. Money was very short. We didn't have much food and as time went on I got big and fat, but I was happy. We did food distribution, taking it to the community centre and down to the pickets. We had hundreds of them. There was a big consignment of clothes came from Belgium and we used to sort it all out. I had to work there as I had a picket, giving out meals in the morning – we didn't have any good experiences with the police. We were always on the road – up to Durham, Nottingham, Leicestershire.

I remember when my mum got involved in the miners' strike, I was seeing this gay man, we were getting married. I was picking up on these ideas about sexuality. I was coming out in my head. And Jean was sitting on there there really excited: what am I going to name them? And when they did come down, they were the most fabulous bunch, really. Everybody had gone out and collected all this money. You didn't believe that people in a big city like London would even care about what was happening to the miners, but they were com ing to help us. I was blown away by them. But I could've come out sooner and it was very scary. Especially the men. They were all very worried that the gay men would fancy them.

But I used to think that I might be gay. But coming to Dulais, I didn't have a partner or a boyfriend, so I didn't need to do what some people did. I remember one woman saying to me, 'oh, Jayne's a lesbian now and she's not going to meet Jimmy Somerville of Bronski Beat,' playing with Richard Coles for their first time as the Communards at Heaven in London. There were paradigm," notes Jackson. "Gay and we came straight back out. I was 16 and I thought, I can't do that! But on another way I was thinking, oh wow! I could've. I say those things but I could shock them. From very early on I kind of had it in my head but I didn't act on it.

It's strange to see Imelda Staunton play Hefina, to be honest, because that's exactly the Ma we had. She was larger than life. It's difficult to describe how she managed it. Stephen Beresford didn't get to speak to her because she had passed away. But he'd done so much research and they had so many people involved during the strike. And I think that because the character in the film has to be the method of the Miner's Strike, they were the right people to talk to. Whoever they had – she had that much thrown at her. Stephen told me he'd been told that a couple of photographs and the costume people asked her what she wanted her to look like and she pointed at one of them and said, "I want to look like that!" My mum never, never could agree anything. But she didn't stand a chance, being told what to do. But I can see it in her, an aunt or someone I know, like that even at 5am in the morning on a picket line.

The making of the film really inspired me. As the LGSM reunion in July, Steph [played in the film by Faye Marsay], who I hadn't seen for 30 years, was on TV. They are all very happy. They cried and I cried. And then everyone in the room started shouting, "Jayne's a lesbian now and this is her partner," and they pulled Emilyn in front of the screen, cheering. I'm so out there now. You can look back and think, what a waste. But first of all I was with my husband for 20 years, my two lads for 18, and I had to stay and then after that, I never had an issue with my sexuality. They grew up with the stories and the posters, the banners, the badges, Coal Not Dole.

Hefina died the day before filming started. I thought she would have liked it because it would've been her family – the first screening he told me was when it was appropriate. The louder the better. Definitely.

"SOLIDARITY HAD A MIRACULOUS EFFECT"

Nicola Field was 24 when she joined LGSM. She also helped set up Lesbians Against Pit Closures.

My first LGSM meeting was a room full of lesbians and other women besides me. There were all these different political organisations represented – the Communist Party, the Revolutionary Communist Party, different parts of the Labour Party – all disagreeing with each other on finer points, which I found quite bewildering. Afterwards, as other women, Kate, who was actually a member of the Socialist Workers Party, came round to where I lived in Deptford, and we decorated a bucket and went to a local gay club and collected some money, and that's how I learnt how to do it.

We were doing all kinds of lesbian-only nights up in town – the Drill Hall, the Fallen Angel and the Bell. I went quite a few times, thinking that people would be hostile because they'd see the women as homophobic but actually there was a warm response and pleading that I had respect. And all the women were feminists too. Women have met people in these clubs – Wendy, Cavan and Polly – who wanted to form a lesbian-only support group I thought, well, this will just increase the number of people collecting money. The men can come in the women's clubs and a lot of the women went to form LAPC and I was in both.

The way oppression was seen then was that individuals benefited from oppression of other individuals rather than as worked out in material class terms. That was a crucial thing because the system benefits from all this oppression, and the struggle against the miners – it was more directed at the gay men. We would look for any opportunity to say why being oppressive, it was quite a wrangling relationship, and I think they sometimes got quite fed up.

I think of that at Lot, gay marriage – we're didn't going and I went to it sometimes – we're sort of coming, these decisions? But at the time black people organised separately, lesbians and gays wouldn't work with straights and lesbians and gays generally didn't take bisexuals. I think it all about. Strangely, once the action phase of the struggle was over it wasn't a action referred to a transsexual woman as a "dolly on the doormat." There wasn't the unity that there is now and I think one of the effects of the Thatcher government's attacks on us and the beginning of neoliberal-ism was that we felt too identify politics, competing with time for who was the most oppressed.

There elements were part and parcel of this time but still we were all fighting the system, and LGSM was one of the wonderful things that came out of that.

Stephen Beresford has done a fantastic job of representing those struggles. He was the lesbian characters point that LGSM is completely non-sectarian and although they are presented slightly as the butt of the joke, they're seen relating very affectionately to the women in the mining community in a completely different way from the men.

Pride is a superb celebration of that solidarity between the working class and LGSM and the youth, Mr Warmington says it doesn't show is what happened to the miners then, and what happens, many struggles and campaigns now – the absolute opportunism of the Labour leadership and many of the trade union leaders, who cosmos the miners supply, and then left them to fight their own fight. And then over the next decade or so after many years of effort by lesbians and gay men in trade unions trying to get personally recognised, it was included in the TUC's equal opportunity because the NUM backed it. And that is a historic example of what can be achieved – ordinary people can stand against establishment enemy that tried this solitary effect to change people's attitudes, and change them fast.

Nevertheless, it's a fallacy that there's no more gay oppression and that the whole population loves lesbian and gay people absolutely now. We've got a text Street. From fashion to pop songs, we're a lot more explicit, homophobic, LGSM is extremely homophobic, young lesbians and gays still face isolation and rejection. And of course we are undergoing a vicious Tory austerity programme. This government is using the bankers' crisis to punish and conquer, which includes public services and community organisations to bits. Many LGBTQ groups are losing their funding, so we've still got a fight on.

Pride tells the story of two intensely characterised parts of the working class movement but we've still got signs of a movement that can come back together uniting and striking together in defence of those previous services – the NHS, education, welfare benefits, housing and so on, and see it as a common fight. I see LGBTQ people organising openly and actively in these trade union fights – a vital and active part of resistance to these Tory attacks, just as we were 30 years ago. ●

Pride is in cinemas from 12 September
Digital readers, click the icon to watch DIVA's exclusive clip from the film

---

"MONEY WAS SHORT. WE DIDN'T HAVE MUCH FOOD! AND AS TIME WENT ON IT GOT LESS AND LESS"

of Dulais, leading to the formation of lifelong friendships as well as previously unimaginable political outcomes, which combine to give the film its considerable emotional weight.

The miners lost their battle and the strike ended in 1985, ushering in an era that would see the destruction of British industry and the working class power base of the unions. And yet, there were extraordinary results too. Thanks to block voting by the NUM, the TUC committed to support lesbian and gay equality in 1985; miners' groups were also vocal allies in the 1988 campaign against Section 28. "Even though we lost, it was empowering, absolutely," agrees Jackson. "It had a revolutionary effect on women involved in the strike. Suddenly they were being asked to speak at meetings, get involved in other kinds of politics. Ordinary mining families were exposed to anti-apartheid, gay liberation – and they were learning on their feet, which is very empowering."

Beresford has made the most of the raw material, fashioning a fabulous, funny, feel-good film from the events of an undeniably grim period. But the story wasn't an easy sell, taking him more than 15 years to attract a producer who agreed on its potential for a commercial audience. "My ambition was to put the people in a mainstream film," says Beresford, explaining that while he has nothing against the kind of gay-interest movies that find success on the festival circuit, "I felt that this story should be taken to all kinds of people, all over the country and all over the world if possible".

So what changed? Beresford suggests that the campaign for equal marriage has opened up "a shared experience, an area in which we touch common ground emotionally", in other words, it has humanised gay people in the eyes of the heterosexual majority, enabling investors to imagine a gay-themed film with mainstream appeal. Whether that makes you wince or cheer, it's a shift that will deliver to cinemas everywhere a story that Mike Jackson feared would die with him: "I deposited the LGSM archive at the People's History Museum in Manchester 25 years ago. What's the point, if nobody knows this history exists? It's just sat there, gathering dust. I used to think that when we all pop our clogs that history will have died. Well, it won't now." ●

Pride is in cinemas from 12 September
Digital readers, click the icon to watch DIVA's exclusive clip from the film

United: Mike Jackson (front row, left) and Jayne Haselden-Mackreth (front, second from left) with members of LGSM and the Dulais community, during the Miners' Strike

Inset: Bill Nighy (top right) as Cliff, Imelda Staunton (bottom) as Hefina. Top right: As Sian Bill Pride, and Charles (left) Dominic West and Imelda Staunton hit the dancefloor

Tickets to the Premiere of Pride
September 2014

For

Mark Ashton (1960-1987)
Gay activist, General Secretary of the Young Communist League and co-founder of Gays and Lesbians Support the Miners, 1984-85

and

Hefina Headon (1930-2013)
Community activist, lifelong member of the Labour Party and Secretary of the Neath, Dulais and Swansea Valley Miners' Support Group 1984-85

The dedication in Hywel Francis book 'History On Our Side'

The 30th Glorious 12th celebration -
handing over the banner -
Jayne reads Hefina's speech from November 1984
14th March 2015

Tickets based on the original design as seen on page 100
Right: the poster for the evening

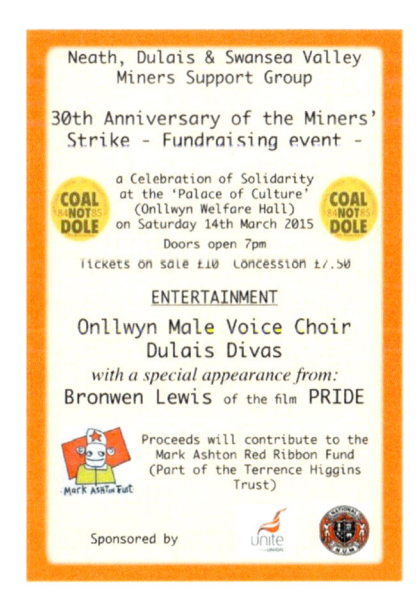

SECTION 3

THE MEMOIRS

In this section you will find the transcripts of family and friends as told in their own words.

Ffion Haf Williams - Aged 7 (Great Grandaughter)

Hen Mamgu ('old' grandmother) used to give me Marie biscuits and tea. She was naughty because she ate Wine Gums and always had drawers full of sweets.

Family

Ian Headon – Son

I remember being in the garden in my car with no wheels with Alison by my side. I can remember my mother telling me off for something. I may have been 3 or 4 years old. That car didn't last long after that. I have more earlier memories of my father than of my mother.

I can remember being in 29 Heol Hen. I remember the television. I can remember Mamgu being there most of the time and mother not. I can remember her cooking pasties and tarts, always making tart on weekends. We went to Skegness in 1964 or 65, miner's holiday camp next door to Butlins which I am not too sure about. I can still remember that holiday, but I do think I was very young. I remember being in a blue Austin van and I know my father changed this van in 1968. This particular van was the one my mother learned to drive in, when they had all the arguments! She was driving along when she pulled over and said "I am never driving again!" I would have been about 7 or 8 years old then.

In the 60s they would go out every Friday and Saturday night. Christine used to come and babysit for us. I am not sure where Jennifer was, but I do remember her coming back with her mates at around 14 years old. I remember being in Seven Sisters school with Jennifer even though she was a lot older than me. Mamgu took me to school not my mother. I didn't want to be there. I do remember how I didn't like it.

My mother used to come up the path from work. She always went out to work early in the mornings and come home late. I used to run to meet her coming up the path. She was always out working.

We were always so close. Terill Phillips lived at the end of the garden, Nana Headon also lived there. Auntie Joan would also be around. I spent a lot of time at Nana's house, making Christmas cake in big tubs for everyone. Wayne Griffiths lived next door to us. I wasn't keen on his mother. His father was called Cyril. I remember one evening when my mother and father came home from the club, he knocked on the door telling them their children had been playing up again! When Christine was looking after us, I was around 10 years old. Jennifer was still at home. I remember I was in the back bedroom with Alison, we slept in the bunk beds. I remember the day they came. They were given to us by Auntie Lillian as Janice and

Derek had finished with them. When Jennifer moved out I got to move into the big bedroom and Jayne shared with Alison.

Life growing up with her as my mother was great, I always remember I had to be singing everywhere.

I am always quite surprised how my mother managed to travel to all the different Post Offices on public transport. She travelled far and wide up the valleys.

My mother used to tell me off all the time. I was always having fights with Alison. I remember once I had terrible pains in my stomach and I had to be taken to hospital. I was in hospital for about 2 or 3 days and she would come there. I never felt without her even when she was working I always knew she was there.

When I was younger, I used to go to Judo with Alison from the age of around 9 to 10.

I used to go up the YMCA at 11 years of age and had to be in at 10 o'clock. If I was late coming home she would tell us off. We didn't have watches so we weren't sure what time it actually was. The YM would close at 9pm, but I think I made it home, sometimes a bit late. I played with a boy called Brynley. He was a bit of a bully and around 4 years older than me. He twisted my arm up really badly once and I fell out with him after that, and didn't trust any of the other boys so stayed at home.

We were a tactile (huggy) family. My mother and father would always be cuddling. I would want to be part of that, and so I would slide down between them to join in. I feel that it's rubbed off on me because I am like that now.

I don't remember David, even though I can remember things that happened before he died but I can't remember him. I grew up with Jennifer around. I remember Jennifer going off to Edinburgh to stay with her father Johnny Smith. I knew my mother didn't like that at all but she had to deal with it. She would let Jennifer go up to Banwen to see her grandparents. We used to ask why Jennifer was called Smith. My mother used to tell us about Johnny. My mother was glad to see her coming home.

When we moved to Onllwyn, the first Christmas we were there, she started to get ill with her thyroid. She was a smoker back then. She used to smoke Embassy cigarettes, she never smoked again after that; although I did catch her smoking a cigar once. A big cigar, her expressive self.

My mother never punished me. She told me off, sent me to my room. My father did, on the other hand. A very different kettle of fish. If I smacked Alison then I would get into trouble, Alison knew how to get a reaction out of me. My father did hit me a few times because I hit Alison.

Both Hefina and John were both grafters. When I look back on what I learned from both of these, what I learned from my mother was community, always very purposeful, always community orientated, working hard for what she believed in.

They were a typical Welsh family to me. Work hard and play hard. They knew how to do this well. They probably had lots of worries but it never reflected on us. I remember there was always Christmas presents and birthday presents. Yes we were a poor family, but we were always going places and doing things, especially clubs.

I was bullied on the bus when I went over the Ystalyfera Comprehensive School. It was a hard year for me in my first year at school. I was in a good set when I started but in my second year I was dropped down to a lower grade. My mother was upset with something in my first year. She didn't think I had done so well because Owen James was in a class higher than me. I remember Valerie Williams was in charge of us, she was the music teacher at the time and looked after us in the library. Mrs Griffiths, one of the deputy heads was a small woman. She walked through the liabrary and asked what class it was. She spotted me. She asked me who I was, I told her. She said "Mrs Williams you must hear this boy sing, I have been in many a place with regard to Blaendulais school, you must hear him sing!" I had to then do an audition for Mrs Williams, who put me in the school choir. I went home that day and got told off for something. I told her "But mam, I'm in the choir." She was happy with that and I got let off. When my voice broke I was able to break away from that.

One Tuesday night, my mother was stood in the kitchen. I had just come home from the YMCA. I came in and sat down in front of the TV. She came in and said "I'd hate to think of a son of mine getting a girl in trouble!" I thought it was very strange as she didn't say anything else but I presume that was my birds and the bees conversation, I didn't even have a girlfriend either. It baffled me at the time, I was 14 years old.

I didn't do too well at school, I went back to re-sit my final exams but it didn't matter as I was already set on going to the Navy. When I was 5 or

6 years old, I remember being taken to Cardiff. We were out for the day visiting Auntie Ruth (known as Auntie Florie) and Uncle Tom and Auntie Dolly and going onto HMS Tiger with my Uncle Tom in Cardiff Bay. I fell in love with that and just knew that's what I was going to do.

At 15 or 16 my mother tried to get me involved as an apprentice somewhere, looking at what I would do once I left school. I was good at Physics and Biology so she looked at these things as a career. My options were mining engineer, fitter and other roles in the mines. My mother got me a test and interview at the Metal Box in Neath, another one at a factory in Cwmgiedd, an interview for an apprenticeship at Blaenant colliery where my father worked and another one at British Rail. I went to them but didn't get offered any of them.

Before I left for the Navy, she had arranged with my father to get another interview for me at Blaenant colliery as a miner. She made me go. I went, but I kept saying I am going to the Navy, she was very disappointed that I wasn't going to take it.

When I left to join the Navy after Christmas, my father told me how much that cut my mother up on that day. She was very tearful. She was so scared of losing me with what happened with David, and I know she was protective of me. Looking back over time and the things she went through around that time, it definitely took its toll on her.

The family came down to Plymouth for my passing out parade, it was a huge event on a beautiful day. Jayne spotted me first and waved at me, and then my mother was popping up and down looking for me on the parade square. I had to march up to meet the captain as I was deputy class leader. I remember Jayne running across and mother following with the camera, so typical of my mother.

We had a family day on HMS Fife. There was my mother and father, Jennifer and Jayne. Jennifer was sea sick on the gangway! On the flight deck going out of the harbour, one of the warrant officers came across. "Hello Dai is this your family?" he said to me. My mother stood up "His name is Ian, I called him Ian so no one could call him anything else!" She gave the warrant officer a right telling off. I never lived that one down.

I always felt like my mother and father were very inclusive people, focused and purposeful in the things they did. They were never bothered by class. She didn't look down or up to anyone. She was always open to everyone who came along and to me that's what community is all about. However, I never understood why she had to be on all of these committees all of the time.

When her father passed away he had angina. He was very ill but there was nothing to suggest he wasn't going to make it. On the day it happened Uncle Dick came up to Onllwyn to tell her. She came in from the Post Office and told us that we had to go down to Mamgu's because Dadcu wasn't well. We knew he wasn't well, but I knew there was something amiss. She didn't want to say anything more than that. We went down to see him. She gave him a big hug and a big kiss and asked me to do the same. She was still trying to mask it.

When Jackie and I decided to marry, my mother organised everything from the Welsh end. They even arranged to pick up a member of Jackie's family on the way. The Southsea Show was on so everyone went to that the next day.

The night that Jennifer died, my mother phoned us the next morning. She told us she had a phone call in the night and had been crying. Jennifer had passed away in America. We had a long discussion, I didn't know how I could console her really as I wasn't there. We went to visit her soon after. We were there for the memorial she had arranged. I asked her "What's the difference between losing David and losing Jennifer?" She said there was no difference whatsoever: "Whether you see your child being ill in a bed for six months or get a phone call in the dark of night, the pain is exactly the same. It hurts, it won't go away, I will feel it forever."

She was a fun loving woman. The Onllwyn Welfare used to be packed with people. When it got a bit dull, she would do something to liven it up, like the time she took out a dildo and placed it in the centre of the table! It certainly got people laughing.

My mother was brilliant with my children. I think she was a fantastic grandmother especially to Christopher as he was older. He was greatly influenced by being down in Wales and thoroughly enjoyed his time. The other two boys were a lot younger so didn't spend much time with their grandmother. She always wanted to be around them, but as she was getting older she couldn't always do what she wanted with them. She always gave them something to play with.

In the summer of 1995, her mother, Katie told her that her time had come and that she had done all she had to in her life. Later that year, her Katie passed away. My mother didn't know how to deal with her own mother telling her this.

When my father died, my mother rang me on the Saturday morning and so I went to Wales with Mathew straight away. She wasn't expecting it. It hit her really badly that he died. A few weeks previously I saw my father, he shook my hand and I knew he was saying goodbye to me. Mother told me not to go to the hospital but to come to the house. We went to the hospital later that evening. We took her down, she made her peace with him, she cried. She was so gutted. She spoke to him and I read a passage out of the Bible. We all said our piece and we left him. "It's my turn now," she said "Nothing here for me now."

I believe she kept on going because she just did, she didn't really have a purpose. I kept saying to her. "Mam, you haven't finished yet, you've still got things to give, you've not done your time yet." Trying to boost her up.

The heart attack nor stroke she had was no surprise to me. I think she was disappointed that she had to overcome them. As far as she was concerned that was her chance to get out. I thought she was a great actress. She was able to cover her dementia really well. She fooled a lot of people. She had it a lot worse than she made out.

Her dementia became very apparent at Auntie Norma's funeral because we took her from Nant club back to Llwynon. She was chatting to us. She told us that her daughter comes to see her, she spoke to us as strangers, asking questions like "Where do you live then? What's your house like?" It was confirmation to me. I knew she would go downhill quite significantly when we took her out of Cae Mawr. It had to happen because she couldn't look after herself anymore. She would have been looking for familiarity and that wasn't happening.

I felt relief when she passed away, just like Jayne. We had discussed this and how her life would pan out once she moved to Ty Mawr. Of course I didn't want it to happen but could I stop it? No. Could I have done anything different? No! Do I miss her? Yes absolutely, I would still like to speak to her. I still try to speak to her all the time.

People forget who you were after time has passed, even in the community. I remember her telling me once, not long after the strike had ended, how shocked she was by people's greed. People were always looking out for themselves. She despised that in people. She wanted to give it all up as she didn't believe that was what community was all about. It was a thankless task for what she did, but she couldn't do anything else. She had to do it.

Her legacy to me has taught me what community is. I can reflect this in my life by the way I am always either in or I am out. If I am committed to work, business, club, organisation, I am all in, I will do everything I can to make that a success. If you lose me then I am gone. I won't be just a small part anywhere if I'm not comfortable with it. All that matters in my life is my family. I can't be a big community person like Mammy was, but if I am involved then I will work hard to make it a success. That's the kind of the legacy she's left me with.

Family

Alison Williams – Daughter

My earliest memory is going swimming with the ladies swimming club once a month with Mami. I was 2 years old. It was Dyfed Road baths pool in Neath. Mami was in the ladies swimming club. Every month the children could go, she was teaching Ian to swim so he would have been 4 years old. She left me at the side of the pool and I saw someone up the deep end. I followed them and jumped in. Next thing I know, I am being pulled out by my hair! My mother had sat me on the side of the pool "Don't move, you are never coming again!" I did go again. I wore a blue bikini with a pattern and yellow binding.

I started school at 3 years old. There were beds in the school where we would go to sleep in the afternoon. We lived at 29 Heol Hen in the corner house with stables across the way and a garage. The land behind was all lumpy and bumpy. We used to ride our bikes over the bumps. Myself and Margaret O'Brian would go out and make mud pies to throw at Craig and Ian!

We didn't have central heating, just an open fire. I remember when the electric used to go off. Mami used to cook toast for us on the fire with her big fork. She used to boil the kettle. One day there were a lot of people there. I touched the kettle and it tipped all over my feet. I remember everyone wrapping gauze around my feet.

We had a swing and seesaw outside the kitchen window. Children used to come in and play as we were the only ones in the street with toys in the garden. The house was used as a walk through and everyone passing through at Easter used to buy us an Easter Egg. Mami used to put them in the parlour with a row each. A row for Jennifer, one for Ian, one for me and one for Jayne. Mami used to buy cardboard eggs and put presents in them as we were fed up of the chocolate eggs there were so many.

At Christmas time the toys were always hidden at the bottom of Mami's wardrobe, I always knew where they were! I shared a bedroom with Ian and we had bunk beds. Jennifer had her own room then. It was extremely cold and we wore socks to bed in the winter. The summer was always long and hot. Our playground was the cemetery and the Cwm. We played as a big gang, with myself and Margaret as the only girls, the rest were boys, Ian, Craig Thompson, Steven Hunt and Steven Thomas. We all played stepping stones in the river. I remember I had to go over the field with Dadi before school to tend to the horses which I really didn't like.

We used to collect nuts, holly and berries and ride our bikes down the dirt tracks. We always had a bike each. Mami always made sure we had bikes. I don't know how she managed to afford that but she always did. Between May and September we would be down at the swimming baths. Mami would give us a plastic bag for our clothes if it rained and a packed lunch. We were given money to have chips from the little blue chip shop owned by Tancocks. The cinema was another place we would visit and have chips on the way home from there too.

My only poignant memory is when my grandfather died, Hefina's father, Tommy. He was my first experience of death in the family. We were living in the Post Office in Onllwyn when Dadcu died. I was 10 years old. Mami went into panic mode. She had received a call from a family member and couldn't shut the shop until 5:30pm. She didn't know what to do. I experienced her in such a state. I never wanted to see a dead body ever again after this. We were made to go into the bedroom to see him on the bed. All the families were there saying goodbye to him. Auntie Verona's family went in first, then Uncle John's family next. Then we went in. He had a bandage around his head to keep his mouth shut and I really didn't like it, I didn't want to see him.

In general I thought I had a brilliant life, a happy childhood. Our mother protected us from any sorrow she was suffering from. I was born in January, 1962 and David died in March that year. That must have been a terrible time for her to have a baby and lose a child. I never saw that sorrow. I not only had one mother, I had lots of surrogate mothers. I had a good relationship with lots of my aunties. I think that's why we didn't have as close a mother daughter relationship as we could have.

I thought my mother was lovely. She used to take me to bed as a small child. She would lay by my side and tell me a story and stroke my hair until I went to sleep. She was a very kind person. That's how I feel about her. She used to give us jelly chunks to eat. She said they were good for our hair and nails!

My friends thought she was a brilliant mother. She was great fun. I had a horrendous teenage life. She was going through the menopause as I was going through puberty. Nothing we did was ever right. We were always at logger heads, Dadi used to come between us constantly. It was a terrible time for me. Auntie Verona always told me to be patient, Mami was going through a bad time with her thyroid, but I didn't really understand what that was. I just knew I wasn't allowed to do anything. When I look back, I was never stopped, I was allowed to go as long as I came home on the right bus. If I did miss the bus, I would be in big trouble with my father.

We would row over me rushing in and going out, going out with wet hair. One day I had gone shopping in Neath with the girls. We had caught the bus and I got off in Onllwyn. I had the time it would take the bus to get to Banwen and turn around before getting back on it to go out with my friends. I ran upstairs and washed my hair. I ran out the back door. She called me back. "You are not going out with wet hair!" I told her to shut up. She was cleaning potatoes by the sink, next thing I knew she threw the bowl of potato peelings over me! As I stood there with the peelings on my head and water dripping down my body, we started to laugh! We always laughed it off.

Mami hated my music, David Essex, Bay City Rollers, Sweet, Diana Ross. I was always told "Turn that bloody music down!" I had a hatred for her then. Ian used to come in and put Pink Floyd and Led Zeppelin on but was never told to turn it down and I resented that.

I can't ever remember being punished by my mother but my father punished me once when I didn't return home on the 9 o'clock bus. He grounded me, however, he took me out on the fifth day and fetched me back that day. I was around 14 years old then. When Mami called me in, I came in. When she said go to bed, I went.

My mother gave me lots of life experiences, she taught me how to work in the Post Office and she taught me the new currency. I was the only one who could work with this after having lessons from Mami. I became extremely good at Maths. In Comprehensive school back in the 1970s it was your parents who influenced the choices of subjects you took. She helped me choose my career path. I wanted to work with children and she supported me with that. She made me take office skills and typing even though I hated it. She told me I could always use it to fall back on. These days, ironically, I work in an office!

Before I got married, Mami went out and bought herself a different dress every week to wear at the ceremony, but she would wear it out on the weekends instead! When the wedding arrived she had nothing suitable to wear! However, she did organise the whole wedding. We had the reception in the Onllwyn Welfare. She hired the crockery, they paid for it all. Myself and Russell paid for the cars. She organised the Pony Club women to make the food; I had Steven Thomas as the chef. Everything was hired. She didn't come with me to choose my dress. I didn't want anyone there. Once I had chosen it though, Jennifer and Mami came to see it. They liked it and so Mami bought it. She also made the bridesmaids dresses and Jennifer crochetted the shawls for the bridesmaids.

The actual wedding was a disaster! At 10:30am on the morning of my wedding Jennifer, her boyfriend Paul and Mami went to Swansea to buy clothes. Jennifer was living in London by then and Paul had left their outfits on the bed at home. I was standing in the house with my father waiting for her. Mami returned, ran upstairs got changed, grabbed Jayne and Claire my bridesmaids and left. Jennifer took out the sewing machine and sewed the hem on her dress as I was leaving with my father. I had to ask the driver to go really slowly to the chapel because my sister was sewing her dress and needed to get there before I did. She made it!

The Onllwyn Welfare hall had experienced a power cut so there was no food ready when we got there. I ended up with a caterpillar in my salad leaves, everyone played a joke on me. They had put flagons of Bow larger under the table for us and they all spilled out over the bottom of my wedding dress. Mami and Dadi arranged a party at the house that evening after me and Russell had gone. I felt let down when I got home that we were left out. I looked out of the window and to my horror my wedding dress was hanging on the washing line. It had been in the Twin Tub that morning, it had confetti stains so she washed it.

My mother particularly helped me through one hardship. When I gave birth to Daniel, I had a caesarean section. This drove Mami around the bend as I had such a bad time. The following two years, I was experiencing terrible pains. She took me to a private doctor and paid for me to have my adhesions taken off my scar. She was so fed up of seeing me in pain sitting on the floor. This happened again after I had Alex. It got worse after having him.

Hefina and John Headon were like two peas in a pod. They were complete opposites but they fitted together. She took the lead. She was a complete Welsh mam, Dadi went along with everything.

When Jennifer died, I was married with one son, Daniel, and expecting Alex, I was 7 months pregnant. We used to go down to dinner on Wednesdays. On one particular day, Mami was making dinner. She sent Dadi up to get us. Earlier in the day she phoned me and told me I was going down for dinner, but I argued with her because I can't eat pork and she had made this for dinner. When he turned up he wouldn't tell me why I had to go. I was so insistent with him, he ended up telling me. He said "You've got to come, something has happened to Jennifer." When we got there she was cooking in the kitchen. I went over to her but she pushed me away. She picked Daniel up, hugged him then let him go to play.

I believe Hefina was a good daughter to Tommy and Katie Lewis. She was very grateful to the both of them for what they did for her when she was younger. She was grateful all her life. I saw the gratitude with Mamgu, she helped her to go back to work with all the children. She visited every day, did her shopping, took them out, not just Mamgu but Auntie Lil as well.

Mami was very bitter when her mother passed away. She went into hospital and they discovered there were a lot of things wrong with her. Auntie Verona and Tessa told the consultant how they felt; they were both nurses. They created an almighty row. They told him to not look at the patient's age. He told them he didn't realise his patient had so much family. Auntie Verona was so angry. Mami had been going down and spending all day with her mother. Auntie Norma came to see her. She said "Vina why don't you go and have a break, go to town and have some food, I will stay with Mami." By the time she returned her mother had passed away. She was so angry that she wasn't there at the very end.

Life for my mother when my father died was horrendous. He died in March, 1999. By August she had a heart attack and at the end of the year a stroke. She didn't have a life after Dadi, maybe a few months. She was lost. She wanted everything to have stayed the same. She tried to learn to drive for a few months but was told not to waste her money by the driving instructor. She stopped going out and going to dances. The illnesses changed her life for the worst.

Once she got ill, she became cantankerous. She changed because she wasn't independent any more. She relied on everyone to take her places. She found it difficult to wait for other people. It usually had to be on her terms and if you were late then you knew about it. She lost her independence. She changed even though she thought she was independent, she did things that were risky. She got herself into situations she couldn't get herself out of.

When I realised the dementia had taken hold, I was numb. When I was sat in the hospital in Tonna. I saw the brain scan and saw a hollow space through her brain. They explained to me that because she hadn't been using the emotional part of her brain, it had just died. I was wondering if that was because of all the heart ache in her life that she had switched off. There was a hole in the centre of her brain. I was flabbergasted thinking how she could survive like that.

The biggest teller of the dementia was when she moved from Cae Mawr. Every single day there was an incident. She was going against advice, never listened to me or other professionals, putting herself and others in danger. She was becoming quite nasty sometimes, making people do what they shouldn't. This wasn't nice for them as they didn't want to be nasty to her. I was being called from work regularly as she had gone missing.

In 2011, she went into hospital as she had septicemia. She had been away in Caewern. She wouldn't allow anyone to bathe or clean her. She was now going downhill. I couldn't go to work as I couldn't bear to see her being in hospital with no visitors in the afternoon, so I visited for 2pm and stayed in Morriston Hospital and went back up in the evening and stayed with her for the whole time she was in. I knew she was afraid of the dark and I didn't want her going through that without me being there in the day with her. I couldn't cope with working. I took time off with no pay. This went on from October until February, nearly six months in total. She did return to Llwynon for a very short period but had to go back into hospital.

When she moved to Ty Mawr, it was the worst day for me. I really didn't want her to go. I hated that day. I spent time with her the first week and they told me not to visit so regularly as it was making it harder for her to settle. I wish she hadn't gone there. She should have come to live with me. I feel so guilty about it. It haunts me. I feel like I let her down.

I miss her so much every single day, but there is a little piece of her in each of her children, grandchildren and great grandchildren. That is the legacy she has left me with, she is forever all around me.

Family

Jayne Headon – Daughter (& Author)

My earliest memory of my mother is of me standing in a bowl of water having a wash down. I must have been around 3 or 4 years old. I remember standing in this bowl, a washed out yellow kitchen bowl with a flannel and a soap dish and a towel on the couch. She is washing me all over before bed, wrapping me in the towel ready to go upstairs. This is my only memory of inside the house at Heol Hen, and of my mother in that house.

The outside of the Heol Hen house sticks in my mind. I used to be frightened of the people who walked down the path, especially men. I thought I was going to get stolen. I used to hide. I had terrible thoughts that they would take me. I remember the garden being very big, and I remember the fields and the railway carriages where the horses were kept. I broke a few of my sister Alison's dolls, her walking doll called Pati Pitta Pat especially; my mother gave me a telling off twice for breaking the dolls legs.

One particularly poignant memory of being with my mother as a young child is the day we moved into the Onllwyn Post Office. It was a lot bigger than the house we had moved from. Upstairs was really big and the stairs were split in two; it was quite an adventure moving there. On the first day, I remember being upstairs with my mother when she put her hand into the open fire place and pulled out a cushion. There were quite a few. They were really sooty and dirty. She was laughing and saying 'dirty buggers'. I was 4 years old. The Post Office was the biggest memory of being a small child. I remember being given sweets from the shop and my mother showing me the money after it had changed to the new currency. We used to sit and watch Emmerdale Farm on the black and white TV at lunch time when she closed the shop. It was always her favourite programme.

Generally my mother was a very big woman. Her presence was very big with a loud voice. I felt very safe with her. Although I was a little afraid of her shouting, she never hit me or smacked me or sent me to my room. I thought I had a good childhood. My brother and sisters were older than me, so I had things passed down to me like bikes and clothes. Everything always started out being a bit too big.

I wasn't aware that we didn't have much money. I enjoyed living at Onllwyn, my mother was always there each day. I remember one day I went to school with my favourite black doll. She was an upright standing doll. The other girls brought in baby dolls. That day my friends wouldn't allow me to play with them because my doll was black, I was very upset, but my school friend Dawn told me to go to the Post Office in Seven Sisters where they were selling a baby doll called 'First Love'.

I went home crying and begging for this doll. Obviously I couldn't have what I wanted straight away, but I cried so much, I'm not sure if Mammy paid for the doll or if Jennifer paid for the doll. However, my mother rang the Seven Sisters Post Office and asked them to put the baby doll behind the counter for me. A few days later I had the 'First Love' doll.

I usually had what I wanted for Christmas. I didn't feel spoilt. I felt free. I used to play outside climbing trees! I had friends in the village, which was very small. I always had a bike and I was always at the Pony Club with my family. I knew they couldn't afford to buy a horse for me as much as I desperately wanted one, but my father always managed to borrow a horse for gymkhana days so that I wasn't left out.

Mammy didn't suffer liars and this was something I would find out at a very early age. It was raining heavily one evening when I came out of Brownies to catch the bus from Seven Sisters to Onllwyn. I think I was around 7 years old. I loved the rain and decided to stand in it and get absolutely soaking wet through. When I got on the bus I thought I would be in so much trouble so I made up a story: The bus driver said I didn't have enough money to catch the bus from Canolfan bus stop and made me walk across the bridge in the rain to the Post Office bus stop where I got wet on the way, he would wait for me there. While I went to get changed, unbeknown to me, my mother had gone out to meet the bus (it used to pass Onllwyn, drive up to Banwen then turn around and go back down to Neath). I heard her coming up the stairs, she had the bus driver with her, I hid under her bed. She and him were speaking to me while I cowered with fear and embarrassment. I had the telling off of my life that day, and have never forgotten the consequences of lying to my mother!

I felt that my mother was a huge part of my life living with her. We used to go away to pantomimes and school trips. She always used to have such fun and everyone was friendly, especially the customers in the shop. I used to spend hours with her in there, playing with the weights, weighing money and sweets. I enjoyed my time there.

We moved to Seven Sisters when I was 8 years old. For me it wasn't such a good place to be. I started to get bullied because of my face (I have a port wine stain birthmark on my left cheek). Some of the families in Seven Sisters didn't like me and ganged up to bully and threaten me.

Again we lived in a house where this time, next door was a thoroughfare, and people used to walk through to the other side of the estate called the 'site'. The girls who bullied me, used to go that way and called me 'patch' and made my life hell.

At the age of 9, I had the biggest shock and surprise of my life. I was playing in my mother's bedroom, putting on her pearl necklaces and clip on earrings when I decided to snoop in her bottom drawer where she kept the family documents. I browsed through birth, marriage and death certificates until I came across an adoption certificate. It had my name on it, and my mother's name was written as Jennifer Smith. I couldn't believe what I was reading. I now had the dilemma of telling my mother I had been snooping in her bottom drawer and found this document, but I was so excited to find out more I ran downstairs and shouted, "Was I adopted?" My mother was very good with me, she was surprised too that I had come out and asked this, but she was calm. As I dressed ready for Sunday School she told me the whole story followed by a very big hug.

My friends at the beginning of our time there were the younger children in the street. We used to form 'gangs' and my mother would let us play in the parlour on rainy days. If she wanted me and I was out and about she used to stand at the corner of the house and bellow my name out at the top of her voice 'JAYNE' – it was like a huge Chinese whisper passed down the village until the message reached me that she was calling. I used to jump on my bike and race home praying that the bullies wouldn't be somewhere along the way waiting to beat me up.

I tried to adapt to living in Seven, but it wasn't so good. As I grew up and went to clubs I never really felt accepted in the village. This made me make wrong decisions a lot. When I joined the Brass Band my mother wasn't best pleased. I came home with a tenor horn. This used to drive her mad, she would shout up the stairs "How much more of that toot tooting are you going to be doing?! You're not going to stick at this". I did, I stuck at it for 10 years! Eventually she joined the committee for the band, as part of her nature, she then helped fundraise and organise events.

My friends in Seven Sisters, ones who didn't know her very well were frightened of her, the boys in the street especially. As I got older, she used to walk down the street on her way home or out to some meeting. I would often be with a gang of boys. She would look at me and say "Who you with then?" and when I turned around they had all ran off and hidden! I am sure she thought I used to spend most of my time alone pretending to have friends! My primary school friends seemed to like her, a lot of them were in the Pony Club, like Sali, Ceri, Sian and Alison, so they saw my mother a little more at discos and at club events. I'm not too sure what they really thought of her.

Hefina was a caring mother. When I was ill, she never left my side. She was the only person I ever wanted to sit by my bedside and look after me. I used to faint when I had a sore stomach, and this made her stay with me.

My friends Karen and Dawn, knew Hefina as they grew into adulthood and got on really well with her. The friends I had at comprehensive school didn't really know her. We travelled far to attend the Welsh speaking school and there weren't many children in the village who went there. They predominantly attended the English comprehensive school in Neath. My friend, Rhian, always said she was never at home. We had free reign to do whatever we wanted.

As a teenager I didn't really have many restrictions. I used to go places with my mother a lot. I walked with my head down, and she made me feel safe, which meant I could go out without fear. I used to attend some meetings with her. I think by the time I became a teenager, I was the last of many, and so she left me to my own devices.

I remember at the age of 14, my mother accused me of sniffing glue! Because she had lost her sense of taste and smell she became suspicious. She shouted at me "Are you sniffing glue?" I never sniffed glue! She said "I will have to believe you then. " I didn't have any signs of sniffing glue so I hoped that she would. I did smoke though, and I'm not really sure if she knew about that.

Hefina was part of the Community Centre committee who put on regular discos. I would be smoking with the boys, until someone would run in and tell me my mother had turned up. Out went the cigarette! I made my way to the dance floor with my friend Karen and danced like there was nothing else going on. She would come in, smile and wave.

I always respected my mother. I didn't swear and I didn't back chat. I didn't rebel. I was able to go and do whatever I wanted. She would be out and I respected that she trusted me and didn't betray that. We did have small arguments, about food mainly, as I got older. I got larger after the age of 13 and she didn't like me being on a diet. I followed a calorie controlled diet but she didn't like the way I didn't want to eat the food she made at the time as it was fattening for me.

My punishment for misbehaving was shouting. That was enough, it used to scare me when she raised her voice; she was a clever woman. She had a knack of knowing if you had done something wrong. I loved her to pieces, she was my Mammy. I was safe in my own house and with her always.

At the age of 16 when the strike happened, I began to spend more time with her again. She wasn't a very tactile mother and I didn't feel that I could open up my heart to her. I felt that she didn't have time, so I didn't burden her with any troubles. We did talk, but she didn't help me much with my school work, however she did get a Maths tutor for me when I was struggling; Christine Powell. Mammy was a great person for spelling and also times tables, but that's all I remember of her helping me.

I have two gripes about the way my mother was. One was her hoarding and messiness. There was never a space to sit, the kitchen worktops were always covered in packets and food. The house always looked untidy.

Also, I wished she was in the house more as I was growing up. I used to get fed up of having to wait for her and also for being babysat.

Every Friday and Saturday night I had to go out to family members houses while my mother and father went out drinking, dancing or to an event. Places like my Auntie Norma's house, with my cousins Melanie and Andrea to entertain me sometimes. Other times I went to my Auntie Mary's to play with Nicola or to my cousin Monica's to play with Helen and the boys. Sometimes I used to sneak into my Mamgu and Auntie Lil's flat and hide there from the warden until my parents would come and pick me up. They were always very late. I would have to climb out of the window. I remember being very fed up during those times and always too tired to wait for them. Sometimes the children would go to their beds or fall asleep and I would have to wait with the adults, late and tired, for my tipsy parents to take me home.

Once I was older, around 17 years old, I used to start cooking oven chips and small pizzas, which my mother would never have cooked. The Rayburn cooker was a great opportunity to broaden her horizons on food, like warming food in the oven. She used to like to put cheese on a metal plate and let it melt in the oven instead of using the electric grill.

Hefina was a very supportive mother as I moved into adulthood. My brother Ian encouraged me to join the army but she didn't want me to do that. I couldn't stay in the valleys and she understood why, and both of them, my Mam and Dad, took me to the Careers Office and down to the station and sent me on my way.

It wasn't long after I left that Jennifer died; it was six weeks into my basic training. That's when things changed between me and Mammy. I passed out in Guildford on the Friday. On the Monday I had to catch a train to Caterrick in North Yorkshire. Within a few days I was told I had to go home on compassionate leave for the service they held for Jennifer. When I got home, my mother was really low and very depressed, something I had never seen from her before. She couldn't speak and didn't eat much. One afternoon she made me some food. She was stood by the Rayburn and became quite upset saying "Why did she have to die?" I left my food and went over to her. I tried to hug her but she became angry and physically pushed me away saying "Don't touch me, go eat your food." I didn't eat my food, I went for a long walk down to the river with Boomer the dog. On my return she didn't ask where I had been. I had decided to leave and go back to my training after the service. She didn't have anything to say about that and let me go. I didn't see her for a while after that. In December 1986 I flew out to Germany. No one could speak about Jennifer for years without getting upset.

My mother didn't support me financially through my adult life but she did try to support me emotionally. In 1992 I had a stillborn baby, Aaron. On the telephone she was a great support to me as I was living in Northern Ireland back then, but when she came out to stay with us after I came out of hospital she fell to pieces. She was distraught that I had to go through a stillbirth like she did with her first child. It even got to the point where I had to ask my husband, Stuart to arrange for the Army Padre (Vicar) to pay us a visit so that she could pray with him. However, with the birth of every other child she supported me physically with them. She would come and stay and help with the baby.

She was a fantastic wife to John Headon. She absolutely loved him but hated the fact that he would drink, especially once he retired. He would drink every night. She couldn't go to bed until he came home. He used to drive her to distraction with his drinking. She supported him, which is very evident with the miners' strike and how she stood by her husband and fought with him. You only have to look at photos of the two of them together and you can tell that they doted on each other. They had a funny relationship. She was 'Hellfire' to him, he used to call her that. She used to shout at him for anything and everything, always nagging. He was a very loyal husband.

When my mother was out and about, she was a totally different woman than you would see at home as a mother and a wife. Outside she would love to joke. Any joke shop she passed she would buy something, like joking poop, and clacking teeth. She absolutely loved being a prankster.

My mother took over my wedding. She made the bridesmaids' dresses and her own dress. She also made the ring cushion and arranged the hiring of the kilts for the little page boys, Daniel, Christopher and Alex. She managed to make the bridesmaid's dress for my friend Lisa in Germany. I measured Lisa and my mother made the dress blind without a fitting. It fitted perfectly. Rhian, my other bridesmaid, visited for her fitting, but only once. She paid for my dress. She arranged for a make up artist to come and help me to do my face as she knew I had issues with this. She made sure everyone was invited and a good handful of her own friends were in attendance too!

When my mother became grandmother to my children she was already a guru at this. When Sean and Owen were small she was still very able as a grandmother, taking them out to the saw mills and on walks and play games and visit the parks, spoiling them with ice cream and sweets. I thought she was a very good grandmother, however when Gregg was still a baby she had already had a stroke and was unwell. He used to stay close to her.

There was one time when she took control over one of my children, Sean used to cry a lot when he was a baby. She was nursing him in the parlour when she decided she would take him for a walk. While she was out she bought a pack of cheap dummies. She sneaked a cup of tea into the room and dipped the dummies in the tea and he was fast asleep. Sean never had a dummy or wanted one after that!

When the matriarch of the family, Mammy's mother Katie Lewis passed away, she was devastated again. I remember the funeral at Canolfan flats. All of Katie's children were at the front, Hefina, Norma, Verona and John with Dennis, Mary and John Headon. The tears flowed. Cousins were there and everyone was sad. She was the last of that generation to go and a huge part of my mother's daily life, caring for her and making sure she had everything she needed. It was the meeting point for the family, we would meet with aunties and uncles and cousins at my Mamgu's house. The end of a very big era, Mammy grieved her mother for years.

When my father died, she became ill quite soon afterwards. She had a heart attack but came out to Northern Ireland to spend Christmas 1999 with us. She was very lonely and sad then and she told me that she didn't want to live any more. Everyone was dying and she had no purpose. She was moody and touchy that Christmas. It was really sad on her first Christmas without Dad. Then a few days later on 1st January, 2000 she had a stroke and things changed for her dramatically.

My mother had to learn to live again after her stroke. In the summer of 2000 she came to stay with us again. By this time we had moved back to England and were living in Dorset. I took her to the hair dressers and took her out and about, but she was very unsteady on her feet. Not long after this she developed a water infection. She was wetting herself and so we took her to the minor injuries unit in Blandford Forum. The doctor saw her and gave her some tablets. We took her home not long after. Her incontinence became a permanence in her life soon after. She was very scared in the beginning dealing with the differences she saw in herself.

I started to realise she had dementia, I didn't realise it would get to the severity that it did. The first time I noticed was on her first day at Llwynon after moving out of Cae Mawr. That night I stayed with her, I slept on the couch and helped her during the night. She thought I was one of her home care staff. In the morning she couldn't tell anyone who I was. I stayed with her for a few days but she kept asking who I was. I used to tell her I was Jayne. She used to swear at me and say she knew who I was, but she would then proceed to tell me stories of Jayne.

The day I handed over the keys to the estate agents for 19 Cae Mawr, I said goodbye to my mother. She never recognised me again after that. My mourning for her began then. I was very saddened by this. She was a woman who was so aware of what was going on being part of the community, to live a life without it was not fair and really sad.

I was upset that I couldn't share things with her. Going through a divorce and wanting to talk to your mother at these times made me realise just how ill she was.

When she was in hospital, myself and Alison had to make a decision to not resuscitate. We contacted Ian and we all agreed on this. I did visit Wales quite often, but Alison was there all of the time for her. My life didn't really change much during this time, nothing to the scale of Alison's life. For me it was a waiting game. I waited for the house phone to ring with the inevitable. I lived on a knife edge waiting.

The day before she passed away, I was all ready for going to Wales, but after talking to Alison and Ian, we decided to wait one more day and see how she was. I didn't sleep well that night. The next day Emily went off with her mother and father, Deb and Mark, who were visiting us and I went off in my campervan. I got the call from Alison during that afternoon. I was half way home, and alone in my campervan. I returned home and told the boys. That evening we went out for a meal, myself, Emily, Mark and Deb. I needed that in order to gather up my thoughts.

I was relieved, if that's the right thing to say. Obviously I was very sad, but I was glad that the life she was living was now over. She wouldn't have liked that life. I knew that she would finally be at peace like she wanted.

The fondest thing that sticks in my mind about my mother was the fact she was a community stalwart. I knew that all my life; people liked her, they respected her. I liked that. She was my mother, and although she was physically distant, she was always there at the end of the phone. She was very family orientated and although she never spoke the words 'I love you,' you just knew she did.

What is my mother's legacy in relation to me? Well, she has me writing a book about her life! The legacy for me is everything that I have written in this book. That pretty much says it all. I am extremely proud of a fabulous woman and miss her every single day.

Family

Russell Williams – Son in Law

I have known of Hefina all of my life. My mother, Eira, went to school with her and they also lived next door to each other on Dulais Road. They were friends growing up and into adulthood.

I particularly remember Hefina from the Onllwyn Welfare Christmas parties and when I was in the ATC (Air Training Corps) in Seven Sisters. I thought she had a very strong personality and was very strict. My impression soon changed when I started dating her daughter, Alison. I soon saw she was a loving wife and mother and devoted her life to her children. She never showed her emotions, you just knew that she loved her family very much.

One of my first direct experiences of Hefina was when I was dating Alison. John was not very keen on the idea. He was just being very protective of his daughter and tried to stop us seeing each other. They used to go out to the Onllwyn Welfare Hall on the weekends when they lived in the Onllwyn Post Office. I used to wait outside until Alison gave me the all clear to come in. One night we heard the gate opening, I thought it was John coming back so I ran upstairs to hide. However, it wasn't John, it was Hefina who had forgotten her bag. I will never forget her shouting up the stairs before she left "Russ it's only me, you can come down now!"

I like to think that she thought of me as a good son-in-law and good husband to her daughter and good father to her grandchildren. She never told me but I knew she thought well of me.

She was very supportive towards me, especially during the strike. We were expecting our first child then. I was a miner working underground at Blaenant Colliery. We had no money and had not long moved into our flat in Onllwyn. Hefina made sure we were ok for food and when Daniel was born, she cared for Daniel and Alison.

Hefina was a good grandparent, she looked after Daniel for Alison to return to work and later when Alex was born, she took him in too. Anywhere Alison and I wanted to go she would have the children for us at the drop of a hat. In fact, I can't think of a time when she said no to us.

As Hefina got older after John had died and she became ill, Alison cared for her. She took time off work to make sure Hefina was looked after. She seemed ungrateful but deep down she knew she needed Alison. When dementia set in it was a cruel time. But we all rallied around making sure everything was done for Hefina. My boys loved her very much and my granddaughter Ffion too. She is greatly missed in our family.

Family

Jackie Headon – Daughter in Law

I was 19 years old when I first met Hefina. It was in June, 1981. Ian took me to the Top Hotel pub. I took to John better than Hefina, he was more friendly and I found her harder to talk to. It was all a bit scary. Later I came to know she wanted Ian to marry a little Welsh girl because one summer, when we went to visit, she told Ian "Oh you should have come earlier because Sian was out in the garden in her bikini!"

I thought she was a very strong woman. I am quite a quiet person and she didn't really take well to that. I didn't think she took too well to any of the 'outlaws' really. We were all very quiet, totally different to the four children who are very chatty.

I do remember when we first visited, she tried to stop us from sleeping in the same room together as she didn't want it to influence Jayne. Once, we came there late at night after being in London seeing Jennifer. We slept on the floor by the fire and in the morning she wasn't best pleased. She didn't know if she could bring Jayne downstairs! Ian told her that there was no way he wouldn't be sleeping with me when we were in Wales. He had been away for six months in the Gulf and if she wanted to see him then she had to let us spend time together.

She was a very supportive mother in law, especially once we had the children. I found it easier to go to Wales then. She took over with the babies, wrapping them up in the shawl and taking them for a walk up the road. When Christopher was taken into hospital with Kawasaki disease (a rare autoimmune disease that mainly affects children under 5 years of age) she came straight down to Portsmouth. They both came and stayed at his bedside the whole time.

She was a good mother to Ian, he was a 'Mummy's Boy!' When we used to go and visit she made his favourite food. Ian never lifted a finger because she did everything for him. I think it was because he left home, she wanted to spoil him.

During the wedding she told us we should invite all sorts of people. The strike was just underway when we got married in 1984. We didn't think many people would come, but a bus load came! Ian adds: "That was the point, Mother told me we need to fill a bus load," and that's why she kept asking us to invite so many people, which would help towards paying for the bus hire.

Every year Hefina wanted us to go to Wales for Christmas, which I found very difficult as we didn't really want to go down then. They used to come to visit quite often, take the boys out to places like the Isle of Wight. She always wanted to cook when she visited. She went straight into the kitchen and took over. She wasn't your typical guest. She used to sit on the corner chair and her knitting would take over the whole corner, surrounded by her things.

When she became ill I didn't really visit much during those years. Ian only went down for the day with one of the boys to visit. The last time I saw a photo of her was her last photo. She always used to be dressed up so nicely with her earrings and her jewellery. I was very shocked to see the white hair as I hadn't seen her for such a long time. She looked very old in that photo.

I saw her at her 80th birthday party and that was the last time I really saw her. I thought how thin she was looking, we were sat with her that day. We all went to celebrate.

On the day she died. Jayne phoned me as she couldn't get hold of Ian. I found it sad. I thought it was also sad because she died before the film, Pride. She never got to see it. I think it affected Christopher more as he spent lots of time there, more than it affected the other two, but of course, it is always very sad when someone dies.

Family

Stuart Meldrum – Son in Law

I was 20 years old when I first met Hefina. My first impressions were of someone who was quite formidable. I very quickly got the impression that it was quite clear who was the central element of the family unit and set the direction for everyone around her.

My impressions did change over time, my initial impression of someone that was quite stern wasn't quite correct. I think that some of that might have been down to how she made a judgement on people when she first met them. Whilst she was open and comfortable in company, I think that she liked to hold people at arms length slightly until she got to know them better. With us being so far away and only visiting fleetingly this probably was extended somewhat.

I always had the impression that Hefina was the dominant element in the family group, that set things out and decided on the direction of travel. I always thought that Hefina was very black and white, in her mind there were very few shades of grey. When she made an opinion on a matter there was no question in her mind that it was the correct one. I also felt that this extended to how Hefina judged those that had a different viewpoint on a subject. I suspect that in Hefina's mind there was no concept that any view that was different to hers could be correct. I don't mean that in a particularly negative way or that she was ignorant to others feelings just that she was very straight forward therefore it didn't enter her head that the different view could be anything other than wrong.

My first experience of meeting Hefina was when we lived in Germany and we were back in UK for a period, therefore we went to Wales to meet the family. I remember we went out for a meal with the whole family, in many ways it was like being interviewed by the whole clan.

I always felt that whilst I was accepted into the family, that it was on the peripheries of the main family. Some of this was undoubtedly because we lived so far away from Seven Sisters therefore the interactions were fewer and further apart than those that lived closer to home. I also think that I was too quiet and introverted for Hefina's taste. I think she was much more comfortable in the company of outgoing people.

I always felt that Hefina was very supportive and willing to assist where she could. No matter where we were in the world I always felt that if she was needed to help in any way she would make sure that she was there as soon as possible.

A particular memory that sticks in my mind is about our wedding day. After the wedding, we were waiting in the car to go to the reception and when asked why we were taking so long to leave, the driver said 'Hefina hasn't said to go yet'. Whilst at the time it was a tad annoying, in subsequent years it became more obvious that this said more about the respect that Hefina was given by many in the village than anything else.

I think she was a very good parent. I always felt that she wasn't particularly keen that we were so far away and that she couldn't be as involved as she would have liked, however, she didn't let that influence things.

All of the stories that I can remember are ones that I was told of about the miners' strike that formed part of the film, Pride. As we lived so far away and I didn't know that many people in the village meant that any stories didn't really have a context for me.

I was always impressed by how straight forward Hefina was and how completely comfortable with her own life she seemed. I also had the impression that if she could influence something there was no question of her not doing so, if she couldn't influence it then it became irrelevant in her mind and not worth consideration.

I was always surprised by the fact that although she spent her life in a small village she managed to do so much, she was involved in everything and if she could support something, whether it was something that she knew about or not she would find some way to help.

When I knew she had dementia, I thought for someone who was always so active and involved in so many things in the community that it was a particularly cruel condition.

When Hefina died, it was obviously a sad day for everyone that knew her, however, I couldn't help feeling that she actually went many years earlier. It wasn't the person that was Hefina to be so reliant on others and not to be able to be as independent and involved in everything that she had been in the community over the years. I always wondered how much she knew about how much was going on around her in her last years. I thought she would have much preferred the family, and everyone else, to remember her not as she was at the end but the person that was known to everyone and was always busy.

Family

Daniel Williams – Grandson (Son to Alison & Russell)

Hefina is known as 'Mamgu' to her grandchildren

My grandparents played a big role in the upbringing of my brother, Alex and me. I never liked being away from them. If my parents were working, we would be there getting cared for by them.

Alex and I used to sleep there at weekends and we would play outside in the wet grass and mud. Mamgu would bring us in at a reasonable time and make boiled egg and soldiers for tea. The evening routine was having a wash in a bowl, with a real bar of soap and a flannel. As much as we were dirty with 'worms' under our finger nails, my brother and I used to hate this part of the evening for the five minutes that it would last. I can still smell the damp flannel and the fresh soap now. "Wash them tide marks away!" she would say as she was scrubbing away at our necks.

Before bed we would have biscuits and a cup of tea. My brother would go up to bed first and Mamgu would wink at me saying "Daniel is going up straight after you". I would smile and know that it wouldn't be long until Alex would be asleep and I'd get to stay up and watch 'Poirot' and 'Prisoner Cell Block H'. By the time they would finish, my Dadcu would be home from the local miners' welfare hall playing bingo. I would purposely stay awake to see him. Mamgu would say "That was clever of you Ian". She often referred to me as 'Ian'. (the name of her son and my Uncle).

As we got older we were allowed to stay up later. The chip van would pull into the cul-de-sac in Cae Mawr and we would share a bag of chips together. Mamgu would always share her fish with us. I remember Mamgu and Dadcu's dog, Boomer. Mamgu would always buy him a sausage but most of the time the chip van man would kindly give Boomer this for free. Alex and I would argue some weeks over whose turn it was to feed him, but Mamgu would always intervene and just feed Boomer the sausage herself.

We went with Mamgu on many trips with the Sunday School and Longs coach company that my Dadcu used to work for. We also visited our cousins in Portsmouth during the holidays. I always enjoyed going places with Mamgu and Dadcu in the car. I always thought Dadcu had nice cars. On one occasion during the school holidays, Mamgu decided she needed some wool to continue with her endless knitting. She would buy this from Swansea market, so we caught the service bus (158) from Seven Sisters to Swansea. During our time in the market, Alex and I persisted in running off or messing around as we did. Mamgu had the bright idea of clutching us by the wrist or hand until we got to the wool shop. This was the time I realised that my Mamgu did not walk, she marched, her arms swinging, clutching our wrists or hands. It's what every child wants when they hold hands, 'the human swing'. Alex and I were running trying to swing but Mamgu would have none of it. We arrived at the wool stall in the market. Before she looked at the wool she bought elastic string to tie around our wrists so we wouldn't run off. This is a funny memory of mine, the elastic was tight around our wrists.

I was an infant during the miners' strike between 1984 - 85. I have only stories that have been told to me and not memories of what happened, or what difficulties were put in front of the hard working men and women of the South Wales valleys. All I remember was the banner that was always up in the parlour of Mamgu and Dadcu's house. It was used on one of the marches through London. I remember seeing a picture of Mamgu stood next to Peter Hain in front of the Houses of Parliament along with other members of the march. When I used to ask about it as a child, my Dadcu would say "That's when we went to London with all the gays."

Family gatherings were always hectic at the house in Cae Mawr. With only a small front room and an adjoining kitchen there was never much room for us all to fit, but Mamgu made sure there was room. She loved to cook us all a Sunday dinner. She would always put one aside for Dadcu who would be up the Double H club, Alex, Christopher and myself would sit in the living room in front of the television watching Formula One Racing whilst the adults sat at the kitchen table. I used to struggle to eat my dinner at times and used to wait for Dadcu to get home. He would warm it up in the oven and add boiling water to the left over gravy. I used to sit at the table and watch him mash his cabbage, swede and potatoes up and mix them together, he used to feed me secretly. One day I felt a big crunch in my mouth as I was chewing on the delicious mashed up veg. It was a piece of a saucer that Mamgu used to use to chop up the cabbage!

I have fond memories of Dadcu. He had a 'Postman Pat' van (this was the LGSM red van donated in the strike). I loved to ride along with him in it. We did a lot togther. He used to play checkers for hours with me and we would count the pennies that he collected in his jar for as long as it took. The jar was huge, so this would take a while. He sometimes would pick me up from school and he would take me to the Post Office across the road and buy me my favourite sweets - Alphabets. I was a teenager when he was taken away from us by cancer. It's one of the most horrible memories I have from being young.

I remember how strong Mamgu was when Dadcu was taken ill and spent a very long time in hospital. After his return from hospital, there was a family wedding in Chepstow. My cousin Sara was getting married. I think it might have been the last time he was home. I refused to go to the wedding along with all the other family members because I wanted to stay at home to be with him. He made me chips that day, his chips were possibly the best chips I've ever eaten!

When I think of Mamgu and Dadcu together, this is the image I have of happiness. They always laughed and joked and the memories I have of the house they lived in are all happy ones. I only wish that everyone could be as happy as they were. They were best friends as Mamgu would tell me many years later when I used to cut the grass for her after Dadcu had gone.

One of the proudest moments was when Mamgu came to watch the ceremony of the 'Presentation of New Colours' at Windsor Castle. As I marched past I could see her through the corner of my eye. It was 2006 and I was serving in the 1st Battalion Welsh Guards in London. Mamgu came with my parents, brother and my cousin Alice, to the castle to watch the parade and have refreshments in the pavilions after the ceremony. The Queen was there along with Prince Charles and Camilla. I think I recall that Camilla even sat and talked with Mamgu for a while. It made me very proud to have had my family there and especially my Mamgu.

Sadly her health deteriorated after Dadcu had gone. It just got worse year by year. First the heart attack, which she recovered from, then the stroke. She dealt with this the best that she could as it had damaged the left side of her body, leaving her eyesight damaged and she became unsteady on her feet. This was then followed by old age and dementia. Even with the memory loss she would still recognise my daughter Ffion when we used to go and visit her in Ty Mawr nursing home. Every time we went to see 'Hen Mamgu', we would bring a packet of wine gums for her to chew on. Ffion loved visiting Hen Mamgu and Mamgu loved to see Ffion too. When she was a baby Mamgu used to knit loads of hats for her, just like she did for all of us grandchildren.

The day she passed away I was away working. I received the news over the phone from my mother. The day before I had been to visit her, so I'm glad I got to see her before she passed. I sat with her for an hour or two and we talked while she drifted off to sleep and woke again. We laughed as we talked and it felt normal. I never thought that I wouldn't see her again after I left that night, but I'm glad she went peacefully on her own with nobody watching her. I know that she wouldn't have wanted that. She was a fantastic, loud and funny lady.

Despite all of her illnesses and medical conditions, I don't think I will ever meet a stronger person; woman or man, in my lifetime. I would be surprised if I did. She coped with a lot of difficult times in her life. I take strength in knowing that I share the same gene pool as her. My mother often tells me "You're exactly like Mamgu you are!" I like being told that, it's nice to think that there's a living part of my Mamgu still living in this world somewhere.

Family

Christopher & Mathew Headon – Grandsons (Sons to Ian & Jackie)

Predominantly told by Christopher:

My earliest memory was at Jayne and Stuart's wedding. I don't remember the day very well. I just remember running around the car park in a kilt. I was 3 years old.

I was quite young when I started going to Wales to stay for the holidays, coming home with a Welsh accent. I used to stay with my cousins, Daniel and Alex. I feel my memories are a bit different than they will be for Daniel and Alex, as I only saw my grandmother two or three times a year, although when I did go, I was there for 2 weeks at least.

The house that Mamgu lived in always reminds me of things being dark and dreary, that's how I always remember it. When we used to go down in the summer, we had proper summers then, and lots of good sunny days when we used to go down the Cwm. The house was always grey and always filled with people. Although I know that house would have been cluttered, as a child it used to keep us occupied. The house was filled with boxes of toys. We were allowed to go anywhere in the house. She kept toys from her own children, like my Dad's garage. We used to play with that and the cars.

Mamgu used to make us all sorts of outfits. I used to love running upstairs and putting on the cowboy outfit. One time she made the three of us Power Ranger outfits. We loved those those and played in them for hours. She used to knit bobble hats for us.

I remember just being young with her. She used to take us for walks down the Cwm to pick wimberries or blackberries to make tart. We would also go swimming, days out at the park and down to the saw mills to play at Gun Smoke with the wooden rifles and guns. We could have opened up a shop with the amount of wooden guns we had. She used to take us down to the Pit in Blaenant to play on the train. I used to love going to Wales as a kid. There were lots of fields to play in. The first thing I remember when we got to the house was that the Cawl (Welsh lamb stew) would be on the stove. Jackie adds: "We didn't know what Cawl was until we went there!"

They used to like Sunday dinner around the table. She always made the house big enough with an extended table top. Ian adds: "It didn't matter who you were or where you came from there was always room to have food. Despite the poverty there was always good food on offer."

How did she fit us all in? She managed. The children would sit around a small table near the television. Sometimes we used to use the parlour to sit too and play.

When we used to go to the village with her, we never got anywhere quickly. Everyone would stop and talk to her, it would take us ages. We used to go and see Mamgu and Lil in the flats, I always had my face covered in tart when we used to go there. I loved the food.

She would get us to drop leaflets in through doors for the Labour Party. I remember from a story Alison told me, of how she would dress up in a fairy outfit and collect money. Everyone would put their hands in their pockets and donate.

My best memory of her is of me and Alex. We were bored and it was raining on a very miserable day. We raided her cupboards for things to eat. She was busy upstairs. When she came down she caught us at it and shouted "Stop eating muck!" That really scared us. We must have been about 11 or 12 years old then. When she got going she was quite scary! We ran outside crying with laughter!

Everyone knew who she was. You could walk around the village with freedom knowing she was our grandmother. My Mamgu is Hefina! She got on with everyone in the village. Everyone knew me, I was the kid with the funny accent (living in Portsmouth). Things didn't change over time in the way that I felt about her. I always looked forward to seeing them all.

Mamgu and Dadcu brought Daniel and Alex down and they took us to Marwell Zoo one day. I remember days out with them when they visited us. I was young then and Mathew and Ashley weren't around. I don't have many memories of Dadcu. He was either in bed or out drinking. He was a quiet man.

When we got to the house, she was always so very pleased to see us all. Cawl would be on, or been done, or rissoles (corned beef hash in breadcrumbs). She just wanted to speak to Dad and know what's been going on or if there was any news. I didn't really understand at the time. Looking back at it, my dad was a 'Mummy's Boy'!

Mathew adds: Whenever I went to Wales to visit, I remember Mamgu would always cook Cawl and Dadcu would be peeling the potatoes in a bowl on the floor. My memories are of Dandelion and Burdock pop and Welsh cakes. I also remember playing in the garden on the front drive. Mamgu had sayings that I will always remember. "Oh that's lovely", "Give in" and "Fair play".

Christopher continues: When I was ill, I went to Great Ormond Street Hospital, and as this was a charity, she signed up to the newsletter. I heard that she still got the newsletter until she moved out of Cae Mawr some 20 years later.

I don't remember where I was on the day she had her stroke. I must have been at Alison's house, but I do remember that she wasn't well after that. The first I can remember was when she had her glasses with her one lens that was frosted.

After that, I remember Daniel's wedding, when she had a walking stick. A little thought went through the back of my head, she was starting to get ill and old now. I went over to see her and she said to me "Who are you then?" I did look different, I had long hair and I was bigger than I had been. Ian adds: "She couldn't get over how different he was, she hadn't seen Christopher for a few years before as he was working on weekends when I had been to visit".

I don't really remember when the dementia set in as she was very clever. Like everyone has said, she hid it well. Alison was telling me some funny stories not so long ago. She told me the story of when Alex and Sarah went to see Mamgu in Llwynon flats. She thought they were the removal men. Alison was telling me that she was clever, getting one over on everyone right up until the end I think. I remember Jayne telling me that she would talk about the miners' strike all of the time. I remember her as a fighter, never giving up. We went to see her in the hospital. From where I remember her being a big lady, seeing her all bony, it was a terrible shock.

The last time I saw her, I knew it would be the last time. My Dad, Mathew and myself went to see her in Ty Mawr. She was even being clever then, we were talking and other residents would be saying "Who is that?" She must have taken a stab in the dark and said "Grandchildren!", because when we were talking to her she didn't have a clue who we were. How she pulled that one out of the bag I don't know, she could have said anything! Myself and Mathew had changed so much since the last time she saw us. She was still very clever at the end.

The day she passed away, I was told by Mum and I had to tell Dad. Jayne had rang the day before and said she may not make it past the weekend. My Dad was asleep. It was horrible having to tell him. I went up and knocked on the door. When he wakes up he takes a while to come around. I wasn't sure if he understood me, I said "It's Mamgu, she's gone, can you phone Jayne?" I gave him his phone and left. I think the rugby was on the TV that day. Dad came down and then just started talking about her.

Obviously I was gutted, but when it was expected, I wouldn't say I was pleased, but relieved that she was out of what she was going through. When I was hearing stories about her going to the shop with no money, it wasn't what I remember of her. It was a relief.

I didn't realise how important she was until she had died. From my memory, there's a scene in the film, Pride, when they come back from London and she flies off the handle. I remember saying "That's her".

Family

Alex Williams – Grandson (Son to Alison & Russell)

I remember my earliest memory is not of being with Mamgu but being with Dadcu who used to drive the school bus. We must have been going on a school trip or swimming. Dadcu must have forgotten something. We went to his house and pulled up outside. I remember Mamgu coming out and giving him his lunch and shouting at him. The bus was full of children. I remember the children asking "Where are we?" I remember telling them it was my grandfather driving the bus and that's my Mamgu shouting at him! I must have been about 5 or 6 years old.

I remember the house being in the cul-de-sac, I remember the ramp and the garage being put in, 19 Cae Mawr. The house was full of clutter, toys, dressing up stuff and old letters. I remember the Rayburn and her tablets all over the place. I remember the bunk beds being in the back room and the whole house being full of toys. It was a great place to be as a child. I have all happy memories in that house.

Mamgu took us everywhere. She looked after us when Mammy was working. We went to Portsmouth to visit Christopher. I remember going to Tenby on community trips and having beetroot sandwiches! They were lovely!

In general I thought my Mamgu was great. I was never scared of her or of Dadcu. I always felt loved by her. When I was in primary school, because the canteen was near the house, I used to go there for dinner. I remember walking to her house was always safe. These days I wouldn't want Ffion walking to the main road, but I was her age at the time and it was safe to do so. I would spend an hour up there for lunch then go back to school to play. It was just me and Daniel (my brother) until he left for comprehensive. I then remember going down to my other Mamgu's (Hefina's mother) for food on Fridays, Daniel and I would play on the stair lift and under the stairs in the old age flats until we got told off!

I loved the food she made. I liked pasty, dinner, ham and parsley sauce. It was grandmother food!

I know she didn't have too much money, she didn't give us much in the way of money. She used to keep 20p pieces in a Smarties tube. I got a tube once, I thought it was great. I had about £3 out of that.

Christopher and I were in her house one day and she was making pickles (onions). This was before she was ill. There was a container of white vinegar and an identical container of white spirit. She made Christopher eat one. He said they tasted wrong, but because Mamgu had lost her taste and smell she couldn't tell. She insisted we ate them anyway. Mammy came down and we told her we didn't want to eat them any more. Mammy went off on one. "Are you trying to poison the kids!?" They laughed about it.

We always had free reign in the house and in the street. I didn't feel like we had any restrictions. It was a safe place to be. We were expected to mow the lawn, Daniel would mow the lawn and I would use the strimmer at around 8 years old.

She bought a climbing frame in the garden for us. She created a space outside the kitchen window for the boys to play. When we were in our teens and visited her house, young kids would still come in and play with all the toys in the garden. They were useless by the time we grew up, all rusty and broken. It was a bit weird seeing other children playing. "Why are these children in your garden playing with our toys?" But it was a happy place to be.

I didn't change my feelings towards my Mamgu when my Dadcu died. I don't really remember the actual day Dadcu died but I do remember the funeral. I was a teenager when Mamgu had a heart attack and a stroke. I don't remember too much changing in my world. When she was in hospital I felt she would be ok. I didn't feel that she was going to die. I believed she would live on.

I remember she wasn't allowed upstairs after her stroke, but I remember every time I went there she would be upstairs. I would ask "Mamgu, what you doing up there?" "Just looking for something," she would say. "How are you going to get down?" I replied, and so she would shuffle down on her bum!

I used to take her to chapel every Sunday when I was 17 years old after passing my driving test. I used to walk her into the chapel. I used to feel proud to be helping. All my old teachers from primary school were there and it was nice to see that I was caring for her. I would pick her up and she would ask to be taken to Ystrad for shopping or to the chip shop to get food. I always had to say no, Mammy used to tell me not to because she was cooking food. She used to try to get me to take her to all sorts of places once she got in the car.

I think she was a very good mother to my own mother. When Mamgu was older, before she moved out of Cae Mawr, Mammy used to come home a bit upset, she would ask her where she had been and why she never visited; even though Mammy went there every day. She was not angry at her but felt as though all the work she was doing went unnoticed. We knew she did and we all took it in turns to check on Mamgu to make sure she was alright. She was always happy to see us. There is a different side to how we knew her as to what her own children saw.

She supported me as I changed and got older. When I went to comprehensive school, she used to ask me about how I was getting on with my school work, but while I was at University she moved down to Llwynon. I remember moving her into the new flats. We were trying to convince her how lovely it was there. It wasn't a care home, it was like and older person's student housing! She didn't like it there.

When she was in Ty Mawr, I hadn't seen her for a few months. I saw that she had lost a lot of weight. I was working away at the time. My girlfriend, Sarah helped me when we visited her in hospital. She used to think Sarah was a home care worker. I remember taking her to meet her and introducing her. Then later she would ask "Where is that girl?" I think she thought she was going to come and clean. She was never sure who Sarah was.

On the day she died, I was working on the production team of the television series, Stella, at the time. We were in the centre of Cardiff, filming in a solicitors office. We could only do this on a Saturday when they were closed. Mammy rang me and told me. I couldn't believe it. I remember being tearful. I told my boss and he let me go home. I drove by myself listening to music. When I pulled up outside Ty Mawr, I saw my mother. I went in to see Mamgu. I stayed there on my own with her for two hours. I chatted to her thinking that she would open her eyes. That's the sort of prank she might pull, then open her eyes and want to escape! I was a lot more upset when I got back home and I took the week off.

My fondest memories of my Mamgu was going away with her on the beach trips. Every trip I remember is being with the both of them, Mamgu and Dadcu. Their house is also part of my fondest memories. I feel the legacy that she left behind for me would be the values and beliefs she had along with her family values. I am not a religious person but I know I do carry some of her beliefs.

    I felt she was a very caring grandmother. She was a typical Mamgu, she was always there. I remember talking to my friends about her. I didn't have any idea about her community involvement or the time of the strike when I was younger. I only found out after she passed away just how much she actually did do.

Family

Sean Meldrum, Owen Headon-Meldrum & Gregg Meldrum – Grandsons (Sons to Jayne & Stuart)

This was a group discussion.

Sean: My earliest memory is of me needing a bath upstairs in Mamgu's house and someone was there, Alison maybe, but I didn't want to get bathed by them. I was kicking up a fuss about it. I went downstairs to tell Mamgu but she told me off. I think I might have been 5 years old at the time.

Owen: My first memory of Mamgu is of us having to pick blackberries for her in the garden into that dangerous bush she had in the garden and down to the place in Pen-y-Banc to collect them.

Gregg: One of my first memories is of her making those little jam tarts. I'm not sure when it was and I know she did it often when we went down to Wales. I also always remember the toys upstairs in the back room. I remember she had a car park toy with a petrol station. I remember taking it downstairs on the floor in front of her facing the TV. I remember her asking me "What have you got there?" and I told her. I remember I played on the floor in front of her a lot when I was young.

Sean: Whenever I think of the house she lived in, I thought she didn't have nice things in the garden. She had a really badly placed set of bars going down the ramp, they used to twist and we used to play with them. I remember the steps in the garden were dangerous.

Gregg: I remember the gate being so rusty.

Owen: She used to have a little white table outside and Sean liked to play with the swingball. The garage was full of stuff. We didn't used to go in there very often.

Sean: I remember a swing in the doorway in the hall. She hung that there for Owen to swing in. There was a notice board on the wall.

Owen: That was a notice she had pinned to the wall. It said something about a woman doing a better job than a man.

Sean: I remember the toilet downstairs before it was made into a wet room. It was a small toilet with lots of tools and spiders and the toilet seat was a soft toilet seat which I felt was weird. In the living room the TV had a strange magnifying glass that made you not see it properly unless you were sitting at the right angle.

Owen: I remember the climbing frame outside. It was so rusty. Once we took it apart and made a slide down the wall instead. I used to fall down the steps all of the time in the back garden.

Sean: Owen, you used to have to wear a bike helmet out to play!
　　I remember my Dadcu being so funny. He would scratch himself so that you would scratch yourself and then he would laugh at you! He had a three legged stool with a star in the middle to put his ash tray and his cup of tea on.

Gregg: I remember the stool, not as Dadcu's as I don't remember him. I used to use it as a table for my drink. Mamgu used to keep her magnifying glass on it.

Sean: Upstairs when the little room had the bunk beds there was so much stuff in the room. We would have to literally climb up the piles of stuff to get to the top bunk. I had a spud gun then.

Gregg: I remember a Christmas tree in a box, this was always in the room. I felt like it never got used but I suppose it did at Christmas.

Sean: I loved it when the whole family met there for roast dinners. I remember Uncle John coming. When I was younger and used to spend time there, she would have us delivering things through peoples doors around the streets, things like flyers and leaflets.

Owen: I remember Uncle John. He used to come to collect her on a Friday to take her up to the hair dressers. One memory that sticks in my mind is of the time Mamgu shouted at me once when my mother had gone out. Gregg and I were playing upstairs one day and she shouted up the stairs at us. I was so frightened I didn't go down for ages.

Sean: I remember when Mamgu came to stay with us over Christmas in Northern Ireland and I remember when she came to stay with us when we lived on camp back here in England. She had to sleep in the dining room downstairs because she couldn't go upstairs.

On our trips out with mum and Mamgu, I can recall how she loved knickerbocker glories from Joe's Ices in Swansea.

Gregg: When the ice cream van came up the screet, she used to give us money to get ice cream for her but she would call it a 'cornet' and we never knew what they were as we called them 'cones'!

Sean: I thought she was a tough grandmother. She didn't really tell us things, like stories about herself. I can't remember having a full conversation with her in my life although I knew that she loved us. I was always excited to stay at Mamgu's. I liked being with the family. Pretty much from me being 12 onwards she was older and sick then. She wasn't so personal anymore, we had to help her to walk and take her places.

Owen: As a grandmother she was already older and ill when I remember her properly. She used to repeat herself and I never really spoke much to her. She used to ask me questions that I would answer and then ask them again. I thought she was a funny woman. I liked her very much. She told me once how she used to be a very smart person.

Gregg: When I remember her, she was also older and quite ill. When I saw her I used to question if she knew who I was. To me she was an old lady who didn't quite know me. I was never scared of her, she never told me off. I felt that I had to do things for her instead of her getting things for me.

Owen: I remember that my mother cared for her. I don't know what kind of mother she was as I was too young to see that.

Gregg: I remember other children would come in the house.

Owen: The door would be open and they would just wander in and play without asking! I thought that was weird, something we weren't used to.

Sean: She used to say the same phrases over again. "You said it!"

Gregg: That's why the book is titled that isn't it?

Owen: "You said it now!" and "Now then" and "Ooops!". When she used to say Ychafi" (it means 'yuk" in Welsh) Gregg wouldn't know what that was, he used to think it was a noise she made!

Sean: She changed when dementia set in. I didn't really want to go and see her when she forgot who we were. I wanted to remember her being the grandmother I had, cooking for everyone, being busy, going places, reading her magazines and doing her crosswords, not this older woman in a wheelchair who didn't know us. I only saw her once and that was on her 83rd birthday when we visited in the van. I remember her being Mamgu, upright, with brown hair and rather big. The next time I saw her she was small with white hair.

Owen: I always knew she was slowly getting ill. We visited, myself, Gregg and Mum visited her in Ty Mawr in the TV room. That was very hard that day. She didn't like it there.

Gregg: I didn't like the physical changes that happened to her towards the end. Even though she wasn't a very able bodied grandmother when I knew her, she was so old and lifeless when I saw her for the last time.

Sean: the day she passed away I was so relieved for her. I didn't want her to be ill and forget everything. I felt it was her time. I had been ready for her to go for a while. I thought it was cruel that she kept living in the dementia life. I feel she lasted too long for her body. I felt that my Mamgu had gone years before.

Gregg: I didn't feel relieved, I kind of felt sad but it didn't affect me too much because I never felt close to her. Of course it was sad and she had now gone and all that I remember of her as a grandmother. However, like everyone has already said it was a relief for her.

Sean: My favourite thing about Mamgu was her roast dinners and her cooking. I liked the family being all together. I feel that was the only time I ever had a full family. It was the only time we had lots of people around us that we were close to.

I think I was always proud of her but I wasn't sure why until the film, Pride came out. I knew she was always respected. I knew everyone knew her from when I was small. I knew she was big in the community. I feel like her legacy has come through my mother to me.

Owen: In her house, she had lots of papers and newspapers. I always spent hours routing through things. I read a lot about what she had done from those papers. I never understood it fully until now, but it all makes sense and I did kind of know. I saw little things of her being in the newspaper. I am proud she was my grandmother. The same as Sean has already said, it has come through my mother.

Gregg: I feel my political feelings have been influenced by Mamgu. I am left wing and have had many conversations about Mamgu and her beliefs. It seems to be quite similar with the stories I have listened to from my mum. I am very interested in everything she was involved with in that respect. However I can only tell people about the film. I always knew she was a community-orientated woman but I have had no direct experience of that. I have had a chance to speak about the film and about my grandmother to my sociology A level group at school. Some students in my class along with my teacher, attended a screening of the film held at the school where my mum introduced the film. Mamgu was a modest woman and didn't brag about what she did in her life. I am proud of her too.

Family

Martyn Bamford, Katherine Bamford Mason & Sara McNamara – Nephew & Nieces (Son, Daughter & Granddaughter of Verona Bamford – Hefina's Sister)

Note: Hefina is known as Auntie Vina to all her nieces and nephews.

This was a group discussion:

Martyn: My memory starts when we lived in Seven Sisters. I remember the house the Headon family lived in just up from Pen-y-Banc. I remember Alison being a baby there. I remember the ponies in the field behind the house.

Kath: I remember that house, there was a footpath going through the garden and because of this I remember Ian, Alison and Jayne (who were really young at the time) getting so many Easter Eggs. I've never seen so many eggs. Everyone brought presents going through, vegetables and all sorts of things. I used to think how very odd, there you were sitting in your house and somebody is walking through your garden! The ponies were in the field behind with railway carriages. There were two ponies I remember, one was Ian's. When I used to get sent down there, I found it hard. Everyone would be speaking Welsh and I didn't know any Welsh at all. Tess (my sister) never kept up the language but she could recognise it and speak it a bit.

I was sent down to Auntie Vina's after my mum had her hysterectomy. She wasn't able to look after me at the time so I went down to Seven Sisters to be looked after. In those days you didn't recover from this type of operation for months and months. I was put in this Welsh school where I couldn't speak Welsh. I stayed with Auntie Norma and Auntie Vina, I was passed around. There was always room at Auntie Vina's. There was always something going on in her house. There was always plenty of chocolate and sweets there, a very busy house.

Martyn: I went to the school there. I couldn't speak Welsh either, although I probably could understand more than I could speak. There were three schools: The infants and the junior and in the middle the Welsh primary school. Although we did go down to stay on occasions. Myself and Tessa were a bit older and stayed at home.

Kath: I remember the bungalow that Mamgu and Dadcu (Katie and Tommy Lewis) lived in. No one was allowed to go up to the attic.

Martyn: I was taken up the attic by Dadcu and shown the typewriter, I have that typewriter now. He was a very educated man.

Sara: Dadcu paid for Auntie Vina to go to Secretarial College and for Auntie Norma to go to study sewing but not Mamgu (Verona). She had to go and work on the trains. She was around 16 years old in 1939 when she went to Barry to work. I remember that he did teach her shorthand.

Kath: Because mum was the oldest, she had a lot of responsibility to look after the younger ones. There wasn't much of an age gap between Katie and her daughter, Verona. Katie would have been around 16 years old when she gave birth to Verona and expected her to look after her brother and sisters.

I remember Jennifer coming up to stay this way when she was pregnant. She stayed at the convent for a short time. Mum and Dad didn't want her to go to Cardiff to have the baby, she did though. Auntie Vina and Uncle John dealt with it brilliantly. It was quite risqué for the time.

Auntie Lil paid for someone else's further education I recall. I think it might have been Jennifer. I think it was so that she could become a comptometer (someone who worked with the counting machines). She insisted that Jen had this training to fall back on.

Auntie Vina got involved with many things, first the Pony Club then it all spiraled from there.

I remember Uncle John (Headon) used to drive a mini bus. He used to drive bus loads up to visit us in Chepstow.

Martyn: I have some film clips, they are 20 seconds at a time. Some of them have Jennifer in them walking down the back of the lane at our house. That was one of the trips when John Headon brought everyone up.

Kath: I remember the swimming baths in Seven Sisters. We all used to play down there. Ian, Alison, Erica, Andrea, me and sometimes Jayne. I have a film clip of that too. I used to love going up the Cwm. I remember John Headon kept his horses up there and we used to visit them, always plenty of sheep too. There were no fences back then. I loved going up the mountains with Erica, Alison and Ian. Ian was a naughty boy! He looked like an Adonis with his blonde hair. We were born in the same year. Erica was my favourite cousin, she was so funny.

Martyn: The horses and sheep used to roam around. We used to go up the Cwm and see the animals. We also used to go up the other mountain and across to Glyn Neath. David was with us then. A huge gang of us used to go. We found an abandoned gold mine up the mountain with a big blanket across the front of it. Then we followed the Roman road at the very top of the mountain that led to Neath Castle.

Tommy Lewis was a very well respected man. Not only was he a fire man and a first aider, he was very community spirited too and worked for the community. He could give lots of advice to everyone and would have encouraged Auntie Vina to be community spirited too.

Kath: My memory of my Auntie Vina is predominantly when she lived at the Post Office in Onllwyn. I always remember there was Pony Club gear everywhere. Saddles in the toilet, there wouldn't be able to get in there and bridles everywhere hanging up.

Auntie Vina was very passionate. I loved her. She loved children and listening to their stories. As I grew up, I realised that the places in the family where Auntie Norma would be and Auntie Vina and my mother, they were just there, like part of your life from the time you were born.

Martyn: Auntie Vina was fun and I always remember Uncle John (Lewis) too used to always be poking fun and messing about with me.

Kath: I loved Auntie Vina's wedding suit, it was a stunning royal blue velvet, so lush. She looked really gorgeous on her wedding day to John Headon.

Martyn: As we got older and when we moved up to Chepstow, we saw less and less of Auntie Vina then.

Kath: I had a very light hearted relationship with Auntie Vina. She wasn't the kind of auntie I would have gone to. She was all about having fun. She always looked bizarre and there was always a hat! She had a wicked sense of humour. I remember children really warming to her. I remember loving her as a proper auntie. There was always food at her house, she was always making cakes and getting us to eat them. It was like being in one big family. It wasn't until I got older I realised we were all in separate families!

Martyn: I remember some stories she told me, about the miners' strike and what she did afterwards. She mentioned she was doing meditation and she did something with the miners' baths in the community. Obviously as I got older I understood more of what she did.

Kath: Mum and Auntie Vina had a lot in common. They used to talk for hours especially on political topics as they got older. I do think sometimes "God help her siblings for having my mum as their older sister, she was a formidable woman", but then I think they were both like that. They would get cross with each other too and both very passionate about different things. Auntie Vina was so proud of my father when he became mayor and when Mum became mayor after Dad had died. We had hundreds of cards from the valleys when they both became mayors.

Martyn: Chepstow was always so far from the Dulais Valley. The M4 hadn't been built by the time we went. It would have taken us hours to get there over the heads of the valley. I didn't go there much at all once I got into my teens. The last time I saw Auntie Vina was at Auntie Norma's funeral I think. I remember sitting and talking to her.

Kath: The last time I saw Auntie Vina was the last time they visited on a Saturday. Uncle John used to bring Auntie Mary and Auntie Vina and sometimes Auntie Norma up for lunch on a Saturday to meet with Mum. They used to meet at least once every six weeks. Auntie Vina stopped coming for quite a while towards the end. I felt her illness overtook her personality in the end.

Sara: As I have grown older I am in awe of that generation, and of all the women in the family. Auntie Vina and my Mamgu, Verona were strong, confident women who were not afraid to speak out for what they felt was right. They fought for the real people of the valley who needed help. In particular, Auntie Vina with her involvement in the strike has made me think that she was a fantastic role model for all of us to have had in our family. I also think that the fact they were miners' daughters made a huge difference. Looking back at what they have achieved makes you re-evaluate your own life choices to ensure that you make what you feel is the right decision not based on other influences.

Kath: When Auntie Vina passed away, I felt like it was a release for her, and for you all. Martyn and Sara both agree.

Family

Mary Lewis – Sister in Law
Christine Woozley & Monica Thomas - Nieces (John & Mary Lewis' Daughters)
& Helen Bankhead – Niece (Monica Thomas' Daughter)

This was a group discussion.

Mary: The first time I met Vina was when I was courting John. I was coming over to Seven Sisters on the bus with John, and this woman got on in Banwen and he said "Oh it's my sister!" I said "Oh, is she?" He replied "Yes she is, she is living in Banwen. She's married to Johnny Smith". I was a bit shocked. Her hair was going a bit grey then. I thought she must be older than John, but of course she wasn't, she was younger than him. It was in December, 1949 when I first met John.

I thought Vina was a great person. I never quarreled with her, whatever was going on, we did it together. Everyone knew her and everyone liked her.

When I first went to live in Seven Sisters, people asked who I was. I used to tell them I was married to John Lewis, but they didn't know him, so then I would explain to people that my mother in law was Katie Lewis, but still people would be unsure. When I said John Lewis was Hefina's brother, everyone would know!

Monica: I always used to tell people that I was John Lewis' daughter, Hefina Headon's brother! They would all know who I was belonging to then.

Mary: I was 17 and a half years old when I got married. We all got married very young back then. Vina and John used to argue an awful lot when they were younger. Their mother told me once that John used to drag Hefina around by her hair like a cave man when they were really small. He was born in 1927 and she was born in 1930. There was only a few years between them.

She was a really good sister in law. She was very supportive. She was always full of fun.

I remember when Vina was still married to Johnny Smith. She was nursing Jennifer at the time. Johnny had hit her. Tommy (her father) was livid and went up to the house and hit him back. Everyone was so angry then about the way Johnny Smith was. Looking back on the times I had encountered Johnny, there was one time Vina had to take over the telephone exchange in Glyn Neath Post Office. I met Johnny Smith that day, he was lazy and didn't help her at all. I didn't much like him. Once they were divorced, the whole marriage to Johnny Smith was wiped out and no one spoke about it afterwards in the family.

When Vina married John Headon she wore a lovely suit. It was midnight blue, or French blue. Auntie Lil made the outfits for the children for the wedding. The outfits were a tan colour. I thought it was not the best colour for a wedding. We all gave John Headon a telling in the reception, "You take care of her!" We all told him.

Christine: I don't remember the wedding but I know I was there. I was a bridesmaid.

Mary: The hats the children wore were like Sherlock Holmes deerstalkers.

Thinking about the relationship as brother and sister when they were older, I remember we went once to a tinsel and turkey evening in Torquay. Vina and John (her brother) started arguing and Verona piped up saying "Those two are like two peas in a pod!" They were both very determined people.

Another time when Verona and Hefina went off on holiday, they took Martin and David with them. They had one week alone and the second week asked me if I would like to come along. They were like school masters. Verona was in the middle of washing with a towel around her neck. She was waving a stick at the boys saying "If I catch you, you'll have it!"

When I think about what kind of daughter Vina was, I knew that she was the one who did a lot. Tommy and Katie were good parents. They would always include me and buy me things to not be left out. If Vina, Verona and Norma had a present at Christmas, I would get exactly the same.

Monica: When I first met my Auntie Vina she came across like a head teacher, until you got to know her and then you realised that's just how she was. She always came across quite stern and we had to behave. When she started laughing it was so loud. I didn't talk much because I did think she was this large figure.

I remember going down to her house once when she lived in Heol Hen. Auntie Rona (Verona) came for a visit. Martin, Tessa and Kath were all there, I think they were staying. I always thought Auntie Vina had a house full.

I don't remember much about David, but I do remember him a bit. It was one day when Auntie Rona had come to stay at Auntie Vina's. Chris, Jen and Tess were all similar ages and I was younger so I was a nuisance to them. I didn't feel so good. David was so gentle, and he was so kind to me that day. He said "Don't worry, a few more years now and you'll be ok." And he was right. He was around 13 years old at the time. He was already ill then. Mamgu used to spend a lot of time with him when he was down in the hospital. David would help anyone. So helpful and gentle.

Mary: He was such a gentle person, you can't say that about many boys. It was so sad!

Christine: I always remember playing with Jen down on the field behind the house in Heol Hen. We went to the same school in Cadoxton.

Monica: I was in awe of Auntie Vina a bit because of her work in the Post Office and the council and things like that. I always thought of her as an authoritative figure. When she lived in the Post Office I always remember Mamgu (Katie Lewis) and Auntie Lil were living with her.

I always associate Auntie Vina with Mamgu more. I think it was because Mamgu used to look after the children like Jennifer and all when Vina worked in the Post Offices. It made sense when she went up to live in Onllwyn for a while when she was ill. Auntie Lil went to Auntie Rona's and stayed at Uncle Tom's house during that time. Mamgu was always pegging out clothes in Heol Hen garden when we used to walk down the lane, which is why I connected the two more than the others.

I know a lot about what Auntie Vina was like from Mammy's stories, up the hair dressers with Diana. (Mary nods and agrees). Edwina Roberts was always there with her as well as Doris Trump, they used to tell some wicked jokes. Mammy used to tell me she couldn't tell Dad the things they used to get up to there or he wouldn't let her go any more! (Mary laughs).

Christine: I remember Auntie Vina very clearly living in the Post Office. I saw her mostly while we were down in Mamgu's flat. She always came across as a very strong character.

Mary: Vina was a very busy person with her politics and especially with the miners' strike.
 I remember a funny story when Vina went up the attic in her house one day. She was messing about up there and fell through the ceiling boards right onto the top of the bedroom door! (They all laugh).

Helen: I always knew her as Auntie Vina, but I remember Mamgu (Katie Lewis) calling her Hefina. I can imagine she was someone you would want on your side, a very loyal friend. She was very articulate with the things she used to do and the causes she fought for.

Monica: She always used to write 'Vina' on her cards and Verona was always 'Rona'.
 I always remember Auntie Vina with brown hair, dyed the same as her own mother. She loved jewellery, such lovely jewellery. She was never without her earrings in. Everything matched her outfits.

Helen: I remember the hair colour. She was always immaculately dressed and always wore brooches. Her laugh was the biggest thing.

Mary: We used to go on trips up to Chepstow in the car. She would knit in the car all the way there! John would take us up to see Verona for the day.

Monica: Auntie Vina used to come to knitting class with us. She used to make the dolls, the painter and the builder and all these characters. Everyone used to be in awe. No one else had the patience to do this. She had to stuff every little bit. I thought she did sewing as well, but not as much as Auntie Norma. She did make her own clothes though.

Mary: I had a suit on once when I saw her, it was purple. She really liked it and asked me to find one. I went to every shop I could but I couldn't find one for her.

Monica: She had a really good life, she used to go to the garden parties with

Peter Hain. She always wanted to be out, even when she was ill she still wanted to go out.

Mary: We had the shock of our life once on market day in Port Talbot. It was a Tuesday and we saw Vina walking there. "How the hell did you get down here?" I asked. We tried to warn her she mustn't go on her own. Alison used to get so worried that she used to go without saying anything to anyone.

Monica: I don't remember ever socialising with Auntie Vina, but I do know that she was always at the Polling Station on Election Day. Anything to do with the election and she would always be there.

Helen: I used to do a lot of work with Julie (my auntie). I think it may have been with the DOVE Workshop at the time. I got to know Auntie Vina as being fun and gregarious, when I was in my mid teens, around 16 years old. Up until then she came across to me as quite authoritative when I was a young child. When I used to play in Cae Mawr, Nicola and Gareth (Christine's children) would be up playing and we would go down to play with Jayne in the street.

Mary: All the children used to go together to the summer school playscheme. Vina was involved with that too.

Helen: I always felt Auntie Vina was very patriotic.

Monica: I always remember Auntie Vina speaking more Welsh than Norma, but Andrea is fluent and was always speaking Welsh to Mamgu, and Alison too. There are pockets of family who speak more Welsh than others.

Mary: It's funny because all of the animals would be spoken to in Welsh!
 She was a strong woman. I never heard her complaining, even when she wasn't very well. When she had her heart attack she was frightened. There was a woman on the ward with her who was throwing chairs in the night. She told me that she was scared, she hid under her bed that night! She had the attack first, then Norma had one and then I was there with angina. The dark and the night frightened her especially after being with

this woman and being helpless in a ward. I believe she must have been terrified!

When she got ill, she used to come to the hairdressers with grazed knees or elbows, she would have fallen again but it never bothered her. She wouldn't say it would hurt her.

Monica: I remember her on the mobility scooter. When I was on duty by the school I would see her on the wrong side of the road I would have to tell her she couldn't be over there. People wouldn't see her coming. She was a danger on that.

Mary: She was very happy with her life the way it was, she didn't know once she had dementia.

Monica: When Auntie Vina was in hospital, I went to see her. I thought she was very good at pretending she knew what was going on. I went in and started a conversation. I thought she didn't know who I was, but once she started answering me I thought she did. Her answers were all right! The only thing that gave it away was the nurse who was attending to a woman opposite. Auntie Vina kept saying 'Who's that woman, what is she doing?' I thought that's not normal conversation. She was so good at that. She had lost a lot of weight and it didn't look like Auntie Vina anymore.

We keep them all alive in our memories. They've all gone now, the four of them.

Family

Dennis Newton – Brother in Law
Erica Jones & Andrea Newton Mills - Nieces (Norma's Daughters)

This was a group discussion:

Dennis: Hefina was popular and well known purely because she worked in the Post Offices. She never changed in all the years I knew her.

I knew Vina when I was courting Norma. We got along famously throughout our lives. We used to go on holidays and nights out together, we were all very friendly people and often went away together from the club 'Paddy's' in Neath.

I remember one trip we went on to Blackpool. Norma and I hadn't long been married. They were all going to Fleetwood market. Norma was proud to buy me a shirt. My size was and still is small. She came back with a size 18 collar! So typical of her. They teased her terribly for that. It was her inexperience. There were 6 years between Norma and Vina. Before we were married, Norma had to go everywhere with Vina.

When Norma was pregnant she became very nervous, she had miscarried and had to be very careful. Vina was very supportive; she was one of the first ones down to the house. She was a very friendly sister to Norma, but she didn't interfere in our lives.

Erica: I remember a story about that time when Mammy was pregnant with Andrea. Auntie Vina came to the window and knocked on it hard, shouting "Norma if you don't get in that bed…" I don't remember the rest but I can imagine how it went, some crazy statement! Mammy told me that story. "I wouldn't get in the bed see, and Auntie Vina was knocking on the window at me!" She must have meant well but came across hard!

Dennis: When Vina married Johnny Smith, we were living up in Martyn's Avenue. They were living in apartments there with Maggie Wonacott. Vina was pregnant and had to get married. Not too long after that time, they went up to live in Banwen with Johnny Smith's parents until they went out to Tripoli to live.

When they came back I think Vina was living in Tan-y-Coed with her mother and father and the two children. Johnny had left her then and John Headon was on the scene. John Headon was school friends with Hefina. They were very friendly with each other when they were younger.

Myself and Norma used to go on the train to Neath to the cinema. We had to be back on the bus by 8pm so that John and Hefina could go out and we would babysit David and Jennifer. Norma used to have a big pan of water and bath the children before bed. There were no bathrooms then. We would read stories to the two of them.

Andrea: I remember we spent a lot of time with Auntie Vina when we were younger, which tells me that she was a very supportive sister to my mother.

Erica: Auntie Vina's house was like a crèche, children coming from everywhere to spend time in her home. We used to spend a lot of time up in the Heol Hen house. I remember the horses; one of them trod on me!

Andrea: My first memory, I believe, is of Auntie Vina turning up with this beautiful baby in a blanket with this huge white bonnet on. I was thinking "Gosh Auntie Vina's got a new baby!" Then a year later I remember my Mammy bringing home a new baby sister. My father and my Mamgu (Katie) came to the school in Daddy's grey Morris Minor. I was 5 years old. Mark Watts and Ian had been throwing snow in my little blue slippers. I remember coming out, and shaking the snow out of my slippers. My father was dressed all smart and Mamgu was in her posh coat saying "Dere 'ma, come on, we've got a surprise for you." I was bundled into the back of the car. My mother was stood in front of the fire with the baby in her arms. I remember thinking how thin Mammy was now. I then had a thought: My mother has just had a new baby and she had a big tummy and now it's gone, but when Auntie Vina came home with a new baby she didn't have a big tummy. I remember sitting on the red leather sofa, and thinking about the beautiful baby who was now my cousin Jayne and I was very confused about the big tummy. That is my first memory of Auntie Vina.

Erica: We always used to go everywhere in the mini bus. We used to go up to Chepstow to see Auntie Rona and the family.

Andrea: I remember a particular trip on that mini bus to Chepstow. John Headon had a little Jack Russell dog who sat on his shoulder on the way. The dog did a poo and myself and Ian, who weren't particularly very good at travelling, started being sick from the smell. The van was covered in dog poo and sick, but we had to keep going on the trip. I remember Auntie Vina shouting "Bloody hell!" She cleaned it all up, then shouted "Everyone back on."

Erica: It was a hell of a trip to Chepstow, it used to take us hours and hours.

Andrea: A distinct memory as a child was of Auntie Vina's Sunday dinners. There were tiny mounds of vegetables. A mound of swede and a mound of mash; arranged on the plate with an icecream scoop, with slices of meat on the side. I used to think "Oh, this ice cream tastes like cabbage!" They were the best dinners ever! I remember the three triangular saucepans that fitted on the one ring. I had never seen these before, they were clever.

Erica: She made the most delicious gravy. They were amazing dinners. There were always loads of vegetables in those dinners and most of the time they were cooked nearly every day. I remember going up to work in the Post Office by 1pm. She used to say "You've only come up for dinner you have!" We would watch Emmerdale Farm then go back into the Post Office by 2pm. Auntie Vina used to make plenty to go around. So the three corner saucepans meant she could make more veg.

When Auntie Vina became ill with her thyroid, Mammy told me to go up and help her in the Post Office. I was 16 years old when I first went up there to work. I didn't really want to do this, even though it became my career. Alison and Auntie Vina used to argue so much, I used to see so much of it when I was up at the Post Office. Alison would come in from school and they would start straight away. I could hear them.

Andrea: My memories are mostly of Onllwyn Post Office, not Heol Hen.

Erica: Auntie Vina was always out socialising within the community. She was never at home. With her handbag and matching shoes, she would be gone to a meeting of some kind.

Dennis: Vina experienced many difficult times in her life. When Jennifer died it was terrible: She was a pillion passenger on a motor bike. Vina was worse after this, more than after David.

Andrea: That's the only time I saw Auntie Vina fall apart, and the first time I saw her as a vulnerable person. Up until then I always thought she was as hard as nails. She was really devastated by that.

Erica: Jennifer was so far away, nobody could go to America. It was such a shock.

Andrea: I remember Jennifer sitting on our sofa and telling us that she loved Portland, Maine and wanted to live there. She was cremated in America and her ashes were scattered on the Maine.
I can imagine this would have been a terrible time for Auntie Vina. When David died she had three other children to occupy her but by this time her children had all left home.
As a daughter to Mamgu (Katie Lewis), I think Auntie Vina was always very good to her right up to the end. She was always there for her.

Erica: My mother and Auntie Vina were very close as sisters. Auntie Rona moved away so they weren't able to see her as often.

Andrea: I think Mammy and Auntie Vina were very close too. She would put her coat on and say "I'm going up to Auntie Vina's" and off she would go. They were in sewing class and did a lot together, as they still both lived in Seven. Mammy always saw her as the supportive sister.
Physically, Auntie Vina was a big strong woman, a stoic woman. She had such a tragic life when you look back. She was such an upbeat person, you would never have known what she had been through. With David and Jennifer dying, I expect she hardened over the years.

Dennis: The legacy of Vina I believe was her time during the strike. She was fantastic. She was politically minded. She supported the community, she went about it in a big way. Especially when the Gays were down, I thought they were fantastic. When they came to Onllwyn first of all, they were Communists and Marxists and very left wing; this suited Vina down to the ground. She was definitely working class. The money they used to send down to us was phenomenal. Donations of food and clothes and everything that came in during the strike was great. Vina was part of all of that. She was inspirational for all of the work she did in the community.

Andrea: She was very flamboyant and I can imagine her and the Gays of London would have got on really well. I don't particularly remember the LGSM aspect of the strike happening. I was away at college at the time. I knew Auntie Vina was doing the soup kitchen and that Mammy was supporting her. Melanie (my sister) knew more about it as she was still living at home at the time. She would have been about 15 years old then.

I was doing lots of visual work and essays about the strike at the time. I was getting brilliant marks at college for it.

Erica: When I saw the marching in the film, I did remember that it went on. But at the time I was busy with my own life just having lost a baby prematurely.

Andrea: I always feel that Auntie Vina thought we were all very special and always right up until she was ill. We used to get Marks and Spencers vouchers for Christmas every year. She always sent birthday presents and cards every year even into our adulthood.

I remember her sitting stance: Legs open, stockings on, flashing silky knickers, bag on the floor, lipstick on, fag in hand! I always remember the lines up the back of the stockings.

Dennis: They all sat like that back then! Auntie Rona and Norma too.

Andrea: I remember the very last thing Auntie Vina said to me. We were in the Nant-y-Cafn Club at my mothers funeral. Alison had forewarned me that she wouldn't recognise me, so I bent over her and said "Auntie Vina, it's Andrea" she replied in her gruff voice, "Andrea! I know who you bloody are mun!" That was so typical of her.

Erica: She said exactly the same thing to me!

Andrea: When she passed away I was devastated. It was tragic that she had lost her mind by that time. It was sad that after Mammy went, they all went like dominoes. They all took her death really badly as she was the youngest. I feel it's so sad that they've all gone now. When I heard that the film Pride was being made, I thought 'Wow'! It wasn't until the funeral, and then at the wake when people spoke about her, that I realised just how much respect Auntie Vina had. I was very proud of her for that.

Dennis: I think Imelda Staunton was worthy of her character in the film, Pride. She played her really well. The mannerisms were uncannily like her. The funny part of the film when she pulls out the vibrator reminded me of a story John Headon told me about one of the grandchildren: They had found a vibrator under the pillow and pulled it out saying "What's this Mamgu?" John thought this was funny and had to tell me one night up at the club.

Andrea: I remember the Welsh wool outfit in the film, but I remember it being a cape! The outfits were fantastic and they really did a fantastic job in costume. The standing ovation at the cinema in Pontadawe, when everyone stood up and clapped, was very strange to see in a cinema and indeed filled us all with pride.

Auntie Vina was quite unique in that she was extremely stern and scary and feisty, but also hysterically funny.

Family

Janice Hacker West – Cousin (on Thomas Idris Lewis' side of the family - Daughter of Maggie, Tommy's Sister)

I remember being 13 years old and going out with lipstick on my mouth and I bumped into Auntie Katie (Hefina's mother). She saw my face and made me go home and wash it off. Auntie Lil too would always tell me I should always have a bit of decorum about me.

In the 60s Mary Street was a hive of activity. The hair dressers shop was always very busy, next to the grocers shop. The salon was Hefina's Friday visit. The 'gang' was always there. The fun they would have! They would be passing jokes around and you would hear about it on the grapevine: "Oh Hefina said this, Hefina said that, there's a girl!"

Gwyneth, my friend at choir, was on the Labour Party with Hefina. I asked her what her memories of Hefina were and she said that Hefina always wanted to dance. She was always on the dance floor once the music started and the gin and lemonade would be there on the side, it was her favourite tipple. Always such fun and laughter.

Antolyn's night club was a great place where the football dinner used to be held. I remember a time when we went over there. She was quite glamorous in those days.

Hefina was a wonderful person to be around, she had this aura of fun. One particular time she was collecting for charities and going around the pubs. She had a stocking and was giving all the men gifts out of this stocking (she had been to the well woman clinic to collect 'gifts'). I can always picture her in the Onllwyn Welfare Hall in the back room where the bar is. She would always have a group of the men around her and they would all be sharing laughter and jokes, she was one of the boys!

One evening we all went to my sister Anne's house to a 'Pyjama Party'. Everyone wore pyjamas and Hefina wore a pink set with hands sewn onto the bum and the boob area! She hadn't seen my sister Beryl for years before this party, they had a long conversation catching up. Great times and good laughs!

When I think of Hefina, I wonder did she ever own a pair of trousers. I never saw her in a pair of trousers. She would always be seen in skirts.

She was always so determined, even in the last 10 years. I often saw her going out on her mobility scooter but not being able to drive it properly and driving Alison mad.

Myself and my sister Anne went to see Hefina in Ty Mawr care home. Anne asked "Do you know who I am now?" She replied "Of course I know who you are!" But I was sure she didn't. Dementia is a terrible and cruel illness.

Family

Janice Lavercombe – Niece (Daughter to Lillian & Dai Cook – John's Sister)

I can't remember how old I was when I first met my Auntie Vina, but it was when she started going out with my Uncle John. I do remember when they got married. I used to baby sit for them when we moved to the housing site. I would walk to Nana Headon's and cut through their house always calling in on my way to Pen-y-Banc.

Over the years whenever I was in Seven Sisters, I would call in. I remember her at Nana's house at Christmas time when we all got together. She always got into the spirit of things and wore a paper hat!

She was a very strong woman with very set opinions and no one would mess with that.

I had left the UK when the miners' strike came to an end so I don't know too much what happened but she was always lovely to me and made a fuss every time I saw her.

I remember her at Dad's 90th. She was over the moon that we had asked her to come and when we gave her a birthday cake the same night she could not get over it. That was such a lovely moment.

The last time I saw her was when I had to put Dad into Trem-y-Glyn. She was at the day care centre and I walked him over to see her. She made such a fuss of him. I did try to find her when Dad was ill but could not.

I thought a lot of Auntie Vina. I will always remember her. Every time I saw her at home she would be knitting toys.

I loved the film. It made me laugh and cry.

Family

Christine Scarratt – Niece (Janice Lavercombe's Daughter)

I was fully aware of my Auntie Vina when she lived in the Post Office in Onllwyn. I always thought she was larger than life, imagining she was 7ft tall. She commanded this authority. As a little girl, she used to put the fear of God into me, nothing nasty but as a child it was a bit overwhelming. She had this presence about her. She was so very loud and had a very wicked laugh.

There were always lots of brooches, coats, handbags and hats surrounding her. I don't remember her being 'normal' as I knew it to be. She used to have lovely hats, I used to think she was like royalty.

My Uncle John was engaged before he got with Auntie Vina. I think her name was Nora, but she didn't stay around for long. She was new to the village and lived in Pen-y-Banc. There were certain things that weren't talked about but snippets of information used to come out now and again!

As I got older I thought Auntie Vina's beliefs were strong. She stood up for what she believed in without a doubt. She was never afraid to speak her mind.

I always made a point of seeing Auntie Vina when my children were born. I used to take them to visit her, she liked to know what we were up to.

The family were very close. They always seem 'altogether' in photographs. Back then we were a really big extended family.

My grandmother ended up being a community councillor because of my Auntie Vina. She encouraged her to join many things and go places together. When Peter Hain went into parliament, my grandmother was with her then with Edwina and a few others.

I always remember she used to repeat herself and say, "You said it!" and "Fair do!" even when it was inappropriate to say so.

She was like a tornado. You certainly remembered her when she was in your presence. If she had something to say she would tell you straight away, she wouldn't care what you thought about her opinion, she would just say it. It was accepted because it was just Hefina!

I remember the Pony Club shows. My old school teacher, David Williams from Glyn Neath school was in the YMCA with my Auntie

Vina. She was involved in so much in all her years. She had a lot to do with the community centre in Seven Sisters. I went up to the DOVE Workshop and she was associated with that too. Even when I had the interview with the community bus service, there was a photo on the wall and I thought "Oh there's Auntie Vina!" Ali Thomas interviewed me. He asked if I knew what they did. I said in actual fact my auntie is in the photo. I feel it influenced my job a little bit.

I used to see her every week when I used to drive the Dulais Valley community bus. I used to pick her up on a Wednesday evening for the over 40's club. She always used to come on the town shopper too. She had a trolley that she could sit on when she went shopping. She stopped dressing nice by then which wasn't like her at all.

We had a party because a few of the family shared the same birthdays. My Aaron was 18, my grandfather, Dai was 90 and Auntie Vina was 79. We made a cake for her too when we knew she was coming. We had this big party. She loved it. She had a little bit of dementia then but hid it very well. She was very dodgy on her feet and everyone made sure she was ok. I didn't see her much after that party.

I was awful sad when she died. From the last time I saw her, she was a shadow of her former self. It was a shock to see how frail she had become, she stopped being 7ft tall. If anyone would know anything it would be Vina. If I needed to know it I could go to her and ask and she would always be able to tell me. I was studying something in the DOVE Workshop, and I had no idea how I was going to find information out for it. I went to Auntie Vina and she was able to tell me, I think it was to do with the Labour Party.

Friend

Mrs Betsy Becker (also known as Mrs McCutcheon)
Life Long Friend & Post Office Colleague

I first joined the Post Office in Cwmgrach on 1st July, 1939. Before coming to Seven Sisters Post Office I used to work on the counter in Neath. I did this for the 5 years of the war.

I knew Hefina from a very young age. I knew her mother, Katie. She used to bring the milk to the house. I knew the whole family really well.

On the 1st August, 1944 Hefina and Iris Hooper both came to work with me in the Post Office in Seven Sisters. We all went there on the same day. It was empty when we took it over so we had to stock it up, filling the shelves with cards and sweets. I trained Hefina and Iris.

We had the telephone exchange in the back of the Post Office and so we all had to learn how to use it. We had to answer the telephone within so many seconds. We used to sleep there. There was an open cast site on the Banwen road who would work all night. They used to call in the night to ask for the time. My father wasn't best pleased. Hefina and my father would tell them off for doing this especially in those days.

The former Post Master came to instruct us on some things. The girls were such quick learners. They had beautiful handwriting. Tom Lewis, Hefina's father, told her "You learn all you can now that you have the chance. This is a golden opportunity for you." Hefina was determined to learn the work properly. Everything was done right and to a high standard.

Only 10 days later on the 11th August, I lost my baby. Hefina and Iris had to pull together and run the Post Office themselves. Mr Harris came up a few times to help.

Iris was shy, but Hefina was sharp and ready for people just like her mother, Katie. She wouldn't suffer fools.

Hefina was so meticulous. We used to close the Post Office on a Thursday for cleaning. She used to clean and scrub the whole place from top to bottom. It was very dusty because we were next to the colliery.

Hefina finished working with me when she went to Tripoli to live with Johnny Smith. When she came back, she didn't work much after having the children. Hefina never came back to the Seven Sisters Post Office. She did relief work for the local Post Offices instead.

I used to pick Hefina up for meetings. We were in the Sisterhood at the chapel when we were on the committee. I was the secretary of that committee.

I went to see her not so long ago, she didn't know who I was I don't think. It's such a shame.

Friend

Joy Howells (Community Colleague)

Hefina was a little older than me and in a higher form at school so I did not really know too much about her at that time.

When Hefina left school she worked at Seven Sisters Post Office and I was very impressed as I was still struggling through my days at Neath Grammar School. Later, our paths crossed on numerous occasions. I knew her family of course as I had always lived in Seven Sisters. Although she was married to John for a considerable number of years, I always thought of her as Hefina Lewis and she probably referred to me as Joy Sherwood.

Hefina became a household name here during the miners' strike. She was a great supporter of the miners' cause and her efforts were very much appreciated. I saw a great deal of her on protest marches and at meetings near and far.

Following the miners' strike, a group of women were interested in a project and Hefina and I were invited to join them. We became founder members of the DOVE Workshop at Banwen even before the building became available for our use. We met in draughty halls until we could celebrate having this grand building at our disposal. This venture went from strength to strength with Mair Francis at the helm and it has given so many women opportunities to pursue a career which would not have been possible hitherto. Hefina and I were committee members there for many years and each was elected as Chairperson on different occasions. We met many notable persons and visitors from near and far who were interested in the activities and the courses of the DOVE Workshop.

Hefina was a faithful member of Soar chapel. When it was suggested that a fellowship could be formed, members of St Mary's Church, Soar, Salem and Bethany Chapels united to form the Cwmdulais Christian Fellowship. Hefina and I became committee members for many years. Hefina was the treasurer.

I was at Greenham Common and I remember a bus arriving with Hefina on. They stopped at Greenham to see the women. The Welsh women used to do the night duty. It was wonderful there. The best moment was one night when we were sat on logs talking, at about 3am in the morning, a girl arrived to tell us the police were out and about. At around 6am police cars and bikes arrived. They started burning the tents down. It was terrible. We went across the road and set a fire up there. There was a gentleman coming down the road while we were on the other side. It was Tony Benn. He stopped to talk to us. I couldn't believe he turned up. He was standing on my blanket. I was on the television that night pulling my blanket from under his feet as he stood on it.

Whilst I was a Clerk to the Governors at the local school, Hefina was a Governor, so once again we saw each other regularly. She was also a Community Council member (treasurer too) and I attended many of those meetings. Hefina was also a staunch member of the local branch of the Labour Party.

At one time, we joined an evening class at the school where Mr John Dunstan, Tutor at Swansea University, gave very interesting lectures. One evening we discussed myths and legends, mediums and superstitions. Most of the class scoffed at this subject but not Hefina and I! Some time previously we had visited the Spiritualist Church at Ystradgynlais to hear a visiting medium. I was astonished when she described an elderly lady dressed in long black clothes with a black cape and holding a drawstring pouch containing her money. She belonged to a drama group and had a chest in her bedroom storing her clothes for her participation in dramas. Hefina and I knew immediately she was referring to Hefina's grandmother, Mrs Phillips. Who else could boast of a relative like that!

From the foregoing you will realise that Hefina was a valuable person in this community. She was very popular and sociable. Although Hefina could be outspoken at times, she was conscientious in whatever she supported in the area. I am pleased to say I knew Hefina and would like to think we were good friends through the years.

On 12th September, 2014 I went to Ystradgynlais Welfare Hall to see the film Pride, and also went to the Gwyn Hall in Neath to see it again. I was very impressed by the film and found it humorous and emotional. I had an unforgettable evening as I met up with old friends of mine and Hefina's, including Sian James and Mair and Hywell Francis. I felt that Hefina was in our midst after seeing her portrayed in the film.

Friend

Valerie James (Community Colleague)

I knew Hefina from a very young age. I am a year younger than her but we went to the same school and played in the village as part of a gang of children together. I lived in Martyn's Avenue too.

Before we went to school, when we were really small, we would go swimming together in a group.

When we were in school, we were taken to the Brangwyn hall. We would have been very young then. Mrs Rees took us down to Neath to do gym in the new building. We were there in our white blouses and navy knickers with handkerchiefs in our pockets. When we were finished they gave us milk and cakes but they put the milk on the radiators to warm. It was awful. We had our photograph taken then. I am directly to Hefina's left in the photograph (see page 76).

The bungalow children of Dulais Road and the children of Martyn's Avenue used to meet in the middle to get together.

When the war was on we had evacuees come to the village. I remember one night we went down the rec (recreation ground) in the summertime. My mother said all the children were missing. Someone told my mother we were all under the viaduct down the Cwm. Hefina was with us then. This girl had come as an evacuee and she was showing us how to do things with bulrushes. She was brilliant. She was making umbrellas out of them. Reggie and Sam came to get us and told us to go home because it was very late.

When Hefina went to the Grammar School with Edwina, I stayed at school and then went on to the technical college.

I remember her being at dances in Glyn Neath and up in the YMCA when we were growing up.

We joined the Labour Party when we were around 11 or 12 years old. In the pavilion down the rec they held a youth Labour party. When we were playing down the rec, they used to bring us in to the pavilion. John Headon was also part of it. They would be telling us about all sorts of things. They weren't throwing politics down us, they were telling us that the miners were working hard and being able to provide all the equipment in the rec for us to play on. They told us the council would give money too. We were told not to come to the rec and break the equipment. It was mainly trying to get us to look after the environment. They also told us that the tap in the cemetery was on a water metre and to be careful as people would have to pay for the mess we made. They told us not to throw stones at the lamps otherwise the council would have to pay, then our mothers and fathers would have to pay more towards the council rates, and rents would go up too.

We used to go to the cinema sometimes. It was split then, half for the boys and half for the girls. Doreen, my sister was working on the boys side and Beryl Thomas was on the girls side. If you wanted to court you had to get there early so that we could get into the middle to be with the boys.

We used to make rope swings. The boys would get the rope from the collieries, and a piece of stick as a swing seat, swinging under the viaduct.

Hefina, Eira Jenkins, Minnie Jones and myself were teenagers. We joined the boys club together (girls were allowed in)! We did craft work there. We would also go on trips to Brecon with the club.

When we went off and got married we all separated and brought up our own families. Women didn't work then, so we didn't see much of each other for quite a while.

I knew Jennifer really well when she was courting my son, Derek. He lost his license at one point so myself, Griff, Hefina and John Headon used to take it in turns to drive them to Swansea to the cinema or Jennifer to work. We saw a lot of her then, but once they split up we didn't see much of her after that.

We were on the council together. Hefina came a few years after me, but this was before the Miners' Strike happened. Hefina did an awful lot in the community centre with us. When the pithead baths closed, we opened it up again for discos. We put a film on for the children. Alan Whitney used to bring the films. We used to leave and go into the kitchen to have a cup of tea while the film played. One evening, there was laughter roaring. When we went in to see what was going on. They were watching an adult film (not a pornographic film) instead of the child's film. Katie was waving her arms shouting "Shut your eyes, shut your eyes!"

Hefina joined the over 40s club where we used to play bingo. She seemed alright when she came there, you couldn't tell she was suffering with dementia then. I believe because she was with her age group she understood what we were talking about. We went to Western Super Mare once. I was on crutches and Hefina wasn't too good on her feet, so we decided to go our own way that day. We needed the toilet and saw quite a lot of people with keys to the disabled toilets. We asked, and they told us to go the information desk where they gave us a key each for the disabled toilets. They work in every toilet that are run by the council around Britain. Then we went on the promenade and had ice cream together.

Friend

Emyr Lewis - (Member of the Community and Committee Colleague)

My late wife, Mair knew Vina very well. John Headon lived in Pen-y-Banc and Mair lived there all her life.

I knew them when Hefina and John were living in Heol Hen, because Mair's parents lived next door but one, number 25 Heol Hen. Mair's parents were fairly elderly, and Vina was a wonderful neighbour, very friendly and helpful.

I knew her through a bit of everything in the community, as a neighbour, then the school governership. She was governor of both schools back then. She was a very good governor, she spoke her feelings.

She also used to socialise in the same places as us, such as the Rugby Club and the Onllwyn Welfare. She was extremely supportive of the Onllwyn Male Voice Choir. She certainly enjoyed her social life. Her and Mair would have great fun when they used to meet. Hefina was a true character.

Hefina was undoubtedly a committed Labour Party supporter all her life. She was with the community council and very involved with the development at the early stages of the community centre, which started off as a converted pithead baths. The local authority took over the community centre afterwards and they commissioned the refurbishment of the building which then housed the swimming pool.

Hefina was guaranteed to attend the monthly Labour Party ward meeting on a Monday evening, she was the treasurer. Without fail she wouldn't miss a single meeting. She was one of the people who really did want to give something back to the village. She had such a huge pride for the village she lived in.

Hefina was very committed to Soar chapel as her parents and her whole family were very involved there. She was fully committed to her heritage and was brought up in a working class background. She never forgot her roots. She was a stalwart in Soar Chapel during the Gymanfa Ganu (singing festival) and kept those traditions up too. Hefina gave me her father, Tommy's sermons to see if I could use them at any time. Soar is closed now. She was one of the members who stayed with the chapel to the end. Vina was very conscientious right up until she was taken ill as far as Soar Chapel was concerned.

My father and mother lived opposite Katie (Hefina's mother) and Lil (Hefina's Auntie) in the flats at Canolfan. I used to go and collect their envelopes first. When Hefina was older, I would go up every Sunday morning to Cae Mawr to see her because she wanted to continue giving her envelope to Soar Chapel.

I met her in so many facets of life, she was just always there. She was so supportive in everything. Our paths crossed so much, it was all taken for granted; we knew we would see each other everywhere.

I could relate to her character in the film Pride. She enjoyed a good time as much as anyone. We had many a good night in Vina's company. The portrayal of her character was nearly spot on. Everyone who knew her said they were extremely upset that she hadn't been well enough and had not lived to see the film.

All her life efforts were to endeavour to improve the lives of those living in the village and the community. It was her constant aim that the next generation would be better off than hers was.

Friends

Ann & Malcolm Hathaway (Owners of the Onllwyn Inn)

As told by Ann:

We came to live in Onllwyn in 1976 when we took over the Onllwyn Inn. It was a very hot July. Hefina and her family were living in the Post Office then. Brenda Davies who lived in the street took me up to see Hefina to introduce us. Ever since then the two of us hit it off, we had the same sense of humour and always found the same things funny.

We always used to stand in the corner of the Inn and we used to laugh so much, everyone used to wonder what we were laughing at. She was a character in her own little way. She would sit or stand and listen to it all. She wouldn't say anything but she would laugh and listen into people's conversations. She would tell me what they were talking about and I would laugh too.

I was always on to Hefina about becoming a councillor. She could have been a mayoress or even an MP, but if she did that then she wouldn't have had the time to devote to all the other good causes she fought for. I do think she should have had an award. Anything that anyone wanted she would get or give to them. She worked so hard for others. She was never in the house. I said to John once "Have you got a clean shirt, love? Fetch them up I will do them for you!"

She was mad on Pony Club, she loved going to Wembley with the club. How she had the energy to keep going I have no idea.

One year the Onllwyn Inn had a float in the Banwen Carnival. We were the Addams Family. Jayne and our son, Gordon were Wednesday and Pugsley, Peter Bartlett was Lurch the butler, we had to dress Dai Bowen up as the woman, Mortisha, because we had someone who let us down. We knew we wouldn't receive a prize, it was just a fantastic time. Hefina loved making the costumes and getting involved in the whole occasion.

Hefina and I were very close friends. We really enjoyed our time together. You always knew if she had something to say, it would be there - bang! Next minute she would be laughing and all forgotten. I never said anything she didn't like. She never spoke about anybody.

She used to come down the Onllwyn Inn on Saturday nights with John.

When we had the lounge done, Hefina came down more often, she liked it in there. She made my curtains to match the seats for the pub in the lounge. I told her one day that the brewery had sent me fabric and I had no idea what to do with it. We were expected to make the curtains ourselves then. Some man had already been up and measured the windows but didn't mention about who would make them. Hefina took the fabric from me and had them done in two days. I paid her afterwards, they were up in no time. I also had a coat and skirt that Malcolm bought me but it had gone too small and too tight over the years. She took them and made place mats for the pub, she used everything, even the sleeves and used the lining to back the mats. They were really good!

One year we went to Blackpool with the brass band. Jayne and Gordon were playing in it then. One time, her and John went missing. We all wondered where they had got to. They came back dressed up, John as a woman with his bandy legs, dress and wig! We used to laugh. Hefina would be dressed up in the pyjamas with the hands sewn onto the breasts and bum area. She made me a set of those and I had a hat to match.

The things that Hefina would buy when we were away in Blackpool were so funny. I went into one shop with her, I didn't like it in that shop, it felt like someone would jump out on you. When I mentioned that, she told me not to be so soft! It was so dark "You're not supposed to see!" she told me. "Keep your hand on your sixpence, because something might pop out!" The things she used to buy in the joke shops and adult shops were so much fun.

After Jennifer died, Hefina would come into the pub. I would ask her if she was alright and she would say yes. I would give her a drink, Beefeater Gin and a drop of lemonade, put it on the counter, then John would come and pay for it. I used to ask her again, she would fill up and say yes. I said to her then "Vina, let it go love, you're trying to be so brave, it won't pay you in the end, you've got to let it go." She told me "People don't realise how hard I've took it." Her exterior showed her as a hard person and she would hide everything. It was so sad to see her like that.

Some time after, I would ask her again how she was but she would be filling up, and say things like, "It's been a twelvemonth now". She would have a sad face for a little bit but someone would come in and cheer her up then she would move on.

She was really good in the Miners' Strike. We could say no wrong about Arthur Scargill, she loved him! We weren't keen on him and when I used to say so she used to tell me "No! He's a good leader!" I would respond with "I'll have my way then and you have your way." "Right oh then," she'd say and that would be it.

If you had any worries or troubles then you were ok when Hefina was around. She would listen and wouldn't beat about the bush, she would help people through.

When we moved back here to Bargoed, we didn't see her much. Hefina brought a mini bus full up to see us in Bargoed. We really enjoyed ourselves and talked about things in the past. It was lovely to see them all.

I saw a picture of her on Facebook not so long ago, she had slimmed down so much and it really didn't look like her unless you looked closely at her face. You could still see Hefina in there but I was a bit upset to see her so different.

Friend

Peter Lloyd - (Member of the Labour Party Seven Sisters Ward)

Swimming club was the first time I remember Hefina. I was on the original set up committee. That was the first contact I had with her. After that it was with the Labour Party. She loved the Labour Party, she was our treasurer, in her later days she handed it over to Gwyneth John. We used to meet in the old Legion hall in Martyn's Avenue. I always remember that if anything was going on she was there first, coffee morning or whatever, or if we were going somewhere she would be the one to organise the mini bus. When we were going to the polling stations she would volunteer to mark off the register, Emyr Lewis would be there first then Hefina would turn up. They would be told to do a two hour stint, but not Hefina she was there all day.

In Canolfan where we held events and later meetings, she was always the organiser and really looked forward to it. When she struggled to get anywhere I would go up to the house to pick her up. I would make sure she was safe going in. She was always eager and keen to get going. If I was picking her up at 7pm she would be on the gate waiting eager to go. She was so supportive, if anyone had a proposal her hand would be the first up to agree.

We held dances at the Double H club, they were great, she enjoyed a tipple and she thoroughly enjoyed herself. We would also have the consituency dinner, held in the Working Mens club in Neath. We wouldn't have to ask Hefina to arrange the transport, she would tell us what time the bus would be coming and then organise all that.

One of the nicest things was when we went down to Port Talbot and she met Arthur Scargill, I was there with her, she was landed. She didn't stop talking about it for months, that was the fight in her.

Once everyone was ready, one of the speakers was trying to say the miners were doing it all wrong. I was stood at the back of this conference and could see a wave of movement down the front. The next thing I saw were a few chaps going across the roof, climbing up, they found a rope up there. While this chap was talking the men above lowered down a noose!

National press wrote "Hooligans in Wales". It could have been a lot worse, I could see from the back that the miners were going to go on the stage and drag him down. But when everyone saw the rope being lowered the heat was off and everyone laughed and it calmed down. I watched Hefina on the stage doing her speech. I was so glad for her.

After this event, she found her voice and she was happier to speak. The standing ovation she received empowered her. She was so proud. She hadn't spoken publicly before this. I always used to push her to become the chair but she always wanted to stay as the organiser.

During the strike, she got up to so much. She was going with the women pickets and broke into the offices in Llanelli, I could sit all night and listen to her stories. I have no doubt Hefina was on the picket buses with the men.

We went on a picket line once when a miner was returning to work at Cefn Coed. There was a chief of police there, I can't remember his name but he came over to speak to Hefina. He asked her why she was there and how she felt about it and they had a conversation about it.

She was always at every event in the Onllwyn Welfare especially if it had a political back to it. She would be there to support the Onllwyn Choir when they sang for the miners.

When we were talking about supporting the miners down here, she never doubted any group, like the lesbian and gays, always welcoming anyone and everyone. She was there all the time and kept on with the strike. I saw so many characters. People that you would always remember standing out as a particular figure. People that you know that were sound. I believe her to have been sound, supportive and recognised.

Howard and I used to check the Labour Party audit for the year. There was never anything wrong, the books were always perfect. We tried to keep her to be the treasurer too but she stepped back from that, and instead she became one of the auditors.

She loved going to Peter Hain's garden party, I think her middle name should have been Labour! When we had the dinners, Peter would always bring guests over and introduce them to Hefina. She stood out. She went up to London to support Peter Hain, a group of women with the miners support banner. The Neath constituency had organised that trip.

She started to wear a red rose brooch, it was so appropriate and she wore it everywhere and was proud of it.

Most of the members of the Labour Party were also community councillors and other things in the village. She felt that she could do that too and did get involved with as much as she could and wanted to.

When we heard about the Playschemes which were popping up all over, we decided to set one up in this village too. This was on the back of the success of the discos we held in the community centre. Hefina was at the helm of this Playscheme project too. After the swimming pool had gone from the village, the children had nothing to look forward to in the summer which is why this was so important. We had organised it all off our own back. After a few years, the council saw that we were being successful so they included us in the programme for the county council.

The meeting would go on, she wouldn't be concentring when she was ill, but if I asked her what she thought she would always say 'yes' and was supportive even without her knowing what was going on. I went to see her when she moved into Crynant. I offered to fetch her for meetings then she decided to stop after that. I know she would have gone to Canolfan if it was still there and attended meetings if she could.

I remember picking her up one morning. Gareth Rowlands from Glyn Neath was being taken around by helicopter visiting the villages. When he came to Seven Sisters, we were all lined up waiting for the helicopter to land. He came out to greet everyone and Hefina was so happy and made up to be greeting him.

Hefina was a village supporter. She didn't attend these events because she wanted just to be there but because she supported the cause and wanted to make sure it happened and went well. Another middle name for her could have been 'Village Supporter'.

She would insist that I take money for petrol, but I never took it. We used to argue over it. I would threaten her if she forced the money on me I wouldn't pick her up again!

She gave me lots of kisses and hugs when I beat Morris Davies of Plaid Cymru at the constituency elections. She wanted to be there for the count, when I won she turned around that evening and she grabbed me and hugged me, she was all over me, so proud of me. She used to canvas and would do the whole site, delivering leaflets. I could do nothing wrong in her eyes.

One thing I can never forget about her, when we talk about the old times, she would always say "There you are then!" It was her catchphrase.

She always said the same thing. She would have a wicked twinkle in her eye.

Friend

Derek Tong ⁃ (Community Centre Colleague)

My experiences with Hefina: I thought of her as a Trojan, that's the only word I can describe her as. She brought her family up. She was a very political person. She was a very Christian woman. That sums it up for me.

The first time I met her was in the community centre. She and Stuart Kemise wanted to buy the pithead baths, but they couldn't, so they rented it from the community council. There was a condition that they would never come back to the community to pay for it. It all had to be done with grants. Stuart and Hefina were so ingenious, they could get money out of anyone. We got it going. At the time, Stuart was working at Ford. They were renovating the canteen there and throwing the furniture out, so he told them to put it in a van and send it up to Hefina to use as furniture for the restaurant we wanted to open up in the community centre. This is how it was done. The two of them were so enthusiastic about it. In the end the community council offered a whirl pool, a sauna, a gym and a café, as well as a basket ball court. 13 bunks were also put into the community centre and used for the youth hostel.

The cost was £1 per session. All the committee had to take it in turns to monitor the place and work there. Hefina was the treasurer. She did all the finances. You could always depend on her, if someone didn't turn up, you could rely on Hefina to come instead. I have no idea how she could juggle it all.

She was very politically minded and the Labour Party was her thing. She was immensely involved with anything to do with the miners. She was extremely active during the miners' strike, food handouts and so much fundraising and organising. We received food and donations from all over, even places like France.

We had a bit of a disaster, some Seven Sisters people can be very unforgiving. Everything came to a stop. We had a meeting, we had no money. Stuart found someone who lived near Parfits garage who was a company director who advised us to go back to school! At the time Stuart was chairman and Hefina was the treasurer. There were so many of us officials, we had to become directors. The café that was situated on the Chemist hill was not happy as we were taking his custom. He made such a fuss that there was another café in the village.

There was a development to come. We had what we called the butter mountain and meat, because the common market developed so much food it became too costly to store, so they let it come back to the community. For once I was ahead of Stuart and Hefina. I was a member of the Red Cross in those days. My father read it in a paper, that you could go down with a pension book or a disablement book twice a week, where you would get a portion of cheese, butter or meat at no charge so that the common market could get rid of it's stock. My father asked me one day why he couldn't have it. So I made some enquiries and went to Swansea where they were issuing it. I told them I had 50 old age pensioners, and asked what I could have. They didn't even check, they let me have what I wanted, so I spent a number of days going through Pant-y-Ffordd village. I gave away all sorts. Stuart found out what I was doing. Seven Sisters was next on the list, and Stuart and Hefina along with Val and others got involved with this.

She was a very prominent character, a charitable person, not with money but very giving of herself. She gave her time, which was vital. We would have committee meetings and she would take the minutes when she was secretary. I would work at the community centre mainly in the evenings fixing lights and doing odd jobs.

The local council had a meeting because there were complaints. Stuart was up in the local council, but they were slamming the centre down when there was the slightest bit of trouble.

Eventually we couldn't have any more money from anywhere, so we had to hand back the keys as we weren't able to go back to the council.

I could always depend on Hefina. I worked for 30 odd years at the Red Cross and if I had flags to sell I would always give them to Hefina. I knew she would sell them for us. Any charity she would support, any good cause, she was there. She was an asset. If there was anyone else like her then the community would be a better place now.

If someone could point out to me anyone else in the valley who has done half as much as Hefina Headon has done for Seven Sisters then I will eat my hat, there has been nobody else since.

I can't praise her high enough. For an ordinary person to think so much of her fellow neighbour was brilliant. She would organise trips, they would go everywhere. It will be a long time before someone else like that comes into the village to do what she did. If anyone deserved an honour, she did. But they are very stiff at giving awards to the valley people.

She was treasurer on the community council, and that's where her and I would be stirring up things between us. I used to wind her up about being a Labour supporter!

My last experience of her was when I took a Christmas card up. I noticed she had gone quite frail, it was very sad to see a giant come down, very sad indeed.

Friend

Carole Westall MBE - (Charity and Fundraising)

My first memories of Hefina would be connected to the Banwen Pony Club and the Welfare club. I'm not sure of the date. She would have had the Post Office by then. I would have been having a day out at the gymkhana with the children.

When she moved down to Cae Mawr, I was friends with her neighbour Eira Tucker. I met her again then, when we set up the Arthritic fund inspired by Michael Rise, a very small child living in the street. He went up to hospital in Tapworth. They were using ice to cool the joints of children suffering with arthritis and they needed ice making machines. So we gathered together to fundraise to buy an ice making machine. We ended up buying more than one. We went around the pubs with buckets to collect.

This would have been around the late 70s. From that little bit of fundraising it seemed to grow for lots of different reasons. Fancy dress was always top of the list, hence why all photos are fancy dress! We used to sell raffle tickets at the Legion Club. We held discos too. Any venue we could find we would use. We would do a charity evening where local entertainer Colin Price would bring guest artists. Hefina always had her book and her pen. She was always the paper lady. We organised many parties. My memory of the Silver Jubilee party is when Eira, myself and Hefina went shopping. We were off to buy Silver Jubilee mugs. They couldn't drive, but I could and they were going to direct me! They sent me up a one way street. I had to reverse all the way back!

One particular trip we went on was a shopping trip. More people came this time, like Iris Bevan and Wendy Austin. There were maybe twenty of us. We would meet the coach in Neath and go over to France on the ferry. Hefina had made pyjamas with hand prints on the breasts and bum! No one knew she had these until Eira appeared with them on!

There was always something going on. Hefina would always find something in her handbag. If anything was to do with collecting money for a good cause and having fun at the same time then that's where Hefina would be.

My first impression of Hefina was someone in authority, maybe because she was always writing and making notes, and I always remember she had a hat. She always looked important. Over the years you got to see the funny side of her. She was a bit like a school misstres, but when you got to know her, she had a much funnier side, yet you had to dig to see this.

The impact she had on me was that she gave me the chance to see that I could do those things too. She made things look easy and told me I could have a go. It opened my life up by being with people like her. My mother was a happy woman and a good worker but she would work in the background, whereas Hefina was always in the forefront. She gave me an insight into the fact that we as women could do other things. We didn't have to be the little house wife. I had more freedom when I learned to drive.

I think she has done a lot of good work. She was willing to get up and be heard. The Arthritic fund we started off spurred us on to support our local clinic. We bought equipment for them: They needed nebulisers.

The work in the strike was an absolute necessity. We had to do that to survive. They would spend hours making food parcels, gathering the food and bagging it up so that every family had a bag. My attitude towards the carrier bags of food in the beginning made some people feel too proud to take them, but I felt that without those food parcels we wouldn't eat. At the end of the day, a bag of potatoes and a tin of corned beef would make a dinner. People would think it was unbelievable. It was never ending. It filled your cupboard up. You would have to top it up, but it did cut your food bill down to next to nothing. They were a God-send.

I was quite surprised when I heard Hefina had passed away. I knew she wasn't well, but you never expect to hear these things, no matter how poorly people are. She will go on forever in our memories. It's people like Hefina whose names always pop up in conversations.

Friend

Iris Bevan - (Community Friend)

My husband Lyn and I met Hefina when we moved to 31 Heol Hen. She explained to us she was there if we needed anything. We moved into the house in 1969. When we met her she was a lively character and always full of fun.

I remember on our first Christmas at the house, we had put the presents under the tree after the children went to bed. John and Hefina had been out drinking that night. They came over with a selection box each. I wanted them to be quiet as I didn't want to disturb the children, but she had brought a bottle round to have a drink and she couldn't be quiet! She was comical.

My son, Christopher was a toddler then and he would go through the fence, Hefina would shout, "He's in here again with Lyn's shoes on!" She used to laugh at him walking about with these huge shoes on.

They moved up to Onllwyn in 1971. When Hefina came back to live in Seven Sisters many years later, I worked in the newsagents. We always had a laugh together. I don't remember ever seeing Hefina sad or depressed. She was always dressed for the occasion. She loved her hats! She was always ready to help anyone.

When Hefina had something to say to you, she would just say it. She never held any grudges and never wouldn't speak to you the next day. Like it or lump it, then forget it.

I remember once when we went out for a meal, there was Hefina, Eira Tucker, Verina Griffiths, Julia Rogers, Gorgina Johns and myself. We dressed up as council workmen in yellow coats. Hefina came as a headmistress with full cap and gown and a cane! We had a laugh and she had many stories to tell. She told us before that she wasn't going to dress up, she told us to just do it. She had all these verses written out that we had to say in turn. We were shocked when she turned up all dressed up after telling us she wasn't going to! If ever you had an occasion when you needed to dress up, you would say, "Hefina will probably have it, go ask her!"

I remember when she was involved in raising money for the miners' strike. They would first have jumble sales and I remember Eira telling Hefina she would keep all the hats back for her to try on! We would always have a laugh and fun but we also got down to the serious task of raising money too.

I remember when we went to Belgium on a shopping trip once, Hefina was with us then. She had made pyjamas with black hands sewn on that Eira put on. We used to have a laugh.

When I was up in Chepstow because I had radiotherapy at the hospital there, I had to go for nine weeks. For the first three weeks I went up, then came home for a week then went back for six weeks. I can remember Verona coming in, I could hear someone saying "I've come up to see Iris Bevan, I don't know if she knows me." So she came in with biscuits and things and said "Now you don't know me, but you know my sister, Vina!" Then she explained who she was to me, about being Tessa Bamford's mother and I remember Tessa from years ago. She told me that Hefina had told her to take in any washing that I had if I needed her to do it, though Tracey, my daughter, was coming up! She was the Mayoress up in Chepstow then. Well from that day on the sister at the hospital was nice to me after that! She came in a few times then and Tessa came too while she was working at the hospital, telling me not to worry.

I remember going to see Hefina when John had passed away. It was "Sit down and have a cup of tea!" She was seeing to me instead of me going up to sympathise with her. She always got on with things and always made you smile.

It was sad when she passed away, she was a real character and I am sure that all who have met Hefina remember how bubbly and full of smiles she was. Someone who left an impact on you. It was lovely to hear they had made a film and people could see what kind of person Hefina was and I am sure that people will still have very fond memories of her.

Friend

Janice Jones - (Parent Teacher Association and Pony Club)

I met Hefina first in Seven Sisters Welsh School – Ysgol Gymraeg Blanedulais. Hefina's daughter Jayne was in the same class as my daughter Sali and they became good friends. Because of this friendship, a friendship developed between Vina and myself.

I can't remember exactly but I believe the first time I met her was in a parents meeting. It was a committee meeting to arrange money making activities for the school. If I can remember correctly, Vina was the chairman. We did many jumble sales together and made quite a large amount of money for the school.

My first impression of her was that she was a larger than life character. She was full of jokes and laughter. She was a born leader and organiser. This was seen in the miners' strike, when she helped organise the food banks for the miners' families.

Later, when Sali and Jayne went to the comprehensive school, Ysgol Gyfyn Ystalyfera, Vina and I were the two parents who represented Ysgol Gymraeg Blaendulais in the committee meetings at the school. On these occasions Vina would travel by bus from Seven Sisters to Crynant. I would pick her up at the bus stop in my car and drive us to the meeting. We were always very supportive in the "Twmpath Dawns" (folk dancing) evenings and in the Saint David's Day "Cawl Cennin" (Welsh leek and potato soup) evenings. Vina and I worked well together.

We also worked well together in Banwen Pony Club. In the annual show we made cakes, sandwiches and teas. Vina always played an important part in the organisation of the food on these occasions.

Vina and I were friends and committee members. However once our daughters left Ysgol Gyfyn Ystalyfera unfortunately, Vina and I saw each other only on rare occasions. I used to see her in concerts in Onllwyn Welfare Club or in school concerts when Alison, Hefina's daughter, was a nursery nurse at the Welsh school in Seven Sisters.

By this time my granddaughter was in the nursery class where Alison worked. I often asked about Vina and felt very sad when I heard she'd had a stroke.

My last memory of her is seeing her in a wheelchair. Despite her illness, she hadn't lost her determination and strength of character. Sadly I didn't hear about Vina's death. I no longer had any contact with Alison and spent a lot of time up in Cowbridge taking my grandchildren to school.

Her character in the film 'Pride' reflects her determination and strength of character.

Friend

Rhian Loosemore - (Jayne's School Friend)

I first met Hefina when I went to stay with Jayne for a weekend during the summer holidays. Jayne and I became friends in secondary school. I just knew her as Jayne's mum at that point.

I didn't really know much about Hefina as typical school girls don't talk about their parents. There are far more interesting things to talk about in school! My first impression of Hefina was that she was a strong, formidable character who always seemed to be out of the house more than at home, as she always had a meeting to go to. I didn't know then what these meetings were about, just that Jayne and I were either home alone or out and about doing our own thing which was great for a young teenager.

As I got older I started to understand the good work Hefina was doing for the community and appreciate her efforts and dedication to the cause. To be honest, I probably still didn't really understand what she was really about until I watched the film 'Pride'. It was then that it hit home to me what she did for the community and how much influence she had on the local people.

There was one time in my life when I was fully involved with Hefina, and that was for Jayne and Stuart's wedding. She sewed the bridesmaids outfits and her own outfit. I was one of the bridesmaids, I went to see her for a fitting and we got on really well. I thoroughly enjoyed being part of the wedding party.

After I saw the film, I can now proudly say that I knew that lady. She's my best friend's mum. Even if, regretfully, I didn't take the time or get the chance to fully understand that wonderful lady, I feel immensely proud to have met Hefina and I am totally impressed with the things she has done in her life.

Friend

Christine Powell (Community Council, Strike, Pony Club and more)

I can't remember when the first time was that I met Hefina Headon. I joined the Labour Party when I finished university because I wasn't too keen on student politics. It was 1979, that's probably when I became fully aware of Hefina as a community stalwart.

The first time I remember being truly involved with her was during trips with the Pony Club. I remember this larger than life woman coming onto the bus with bags full of sandwiches. As time went on I realised exactly who she was. It would have been in 1981, we went on the bus to Wembley when Banwen Pony Club made it through to the final round of the Prince Philip Cup games. We completely took over the squash club in the evening after we won, I can remember being in there with Hefina and John and Arfon, singing Welsh songs because we had won the cup. That's the first complete thing I remember.

When the strike happened in 1984, it was all full on then. We used to pick John and Hefina up on a Saturday evening and go up to Onllwyn Welfare for a few drinks. Then we would give them a lift home whatever time we were kicked out!

If you asked me what was important about the strike, I think the fact that all the things we were saying at the time were true, and we were vindicated. The gays and lesbians were an important part, especially with the donation of the van, but there was also a significance of what we had done for them too. I can remember the day they came down to the Onllwyn Welfare. We were on strike a while before they came to us. We were having support from other places too.

It was before Christmas when the money came in from the LGSM. We were well established as a support group by then. In one meeting, Dai Donovan stood up and spoke and told us about his trip to London where he had met a new support group who had money for us. He said the name 'Lesbians and Gays Support the Miners' and I remember the silence in the room. Dai got all defensive! We sent a letter of thanks. A few weeks later they came down. Three stayed with us. Our dog, Butch made a huge fuss of them. One of them said "How do you feel about a bunch of queers coming to stay?" Apart from the vegetarian issue it was all good, I thought "I can handle them being gay no problem, but what do I do with a vegetarian?" Everything was fine. They stood out, it was strange. Everyone in our village had long hair and sideburns, but the LGSM had good hair styles and nice clothes.

Quite often after the strike had ended, Mike Jackson and a few others used to come down. We would go for a pint with them in Onllwyn. The kind of relationship we had with them was so friendly. We would insist on buying them drinks as the miners were now back in work.

I didn't go to many places because I was working, but I know Sian James and Hefina went to an awful lot of places. I took a lot of photos when I did go.

I remember one time we were coming back from the Hay Festival. We had been drinking. We were in the cars and a police car started following us and flashing their lights. We had left two of the boys behind and they were in the police car!

When I watched the film, Pride, and saw the scene when they were counting the money in the Welfare, Stuart and I looked at each other, that was me and him with our dog Butch, on a Sunday night in the back bedroom. We would tip all the money out and bag it all up, then go for a pint in the Bryn pub. Then on a Tuesday morning, Stuart and Butch would take the money up to the Lloyds bank in Seven Sisters.

Hefina was a big part of my life. I remember buttering bread with her so often, the part with Imelda Staunton and Bill Nighy (Hefina and Cliff) in the film reminded me of that. I ended up in Hefina's kitchen so often, boiling hot next to that Rayburn with a mug of tea in my hand, crying my eyes out because she understood. When I saw the scene in the film it brought it back. These were the times when you saw a deeper side of Hefina, her empathy came out then.

When myself and Hefina were in the community council together, I fell pregnant. It wasn't really meant to happen, I was 34 years old. I felt too intelligent for my own good. I felt older and scared from all the things I had read. I remember my father saying something in the meeting. Hefina said to me "I am glad for you if you are glad". She could see it, she was very perceptive like that. She knew me and she could see from my face how

I was feeling about things. There's a couple of times in my life that she's picked up on things with me.

As Hefina got older, I remember a time when we were at the first Dulais Valley show that we held in 2000. There were no toilets up on the top of the tip, she came over to me and told me she needed to go. I told her to go into the lorry, as we had a portable toilet. She went in and without me thinking I automatically locked the door then went off to do something. When I came back about 10 minutes later, she was still stuck in the toilet because I had locked her in. She was shouting out. The toilets were a bit claustrophobic especially in horse lorries!

In March 2014, I was interviewed a few times because of the 30th anniversary of the strike. Jason Mohamed, a researcher phoned me and we chatted. It was about the support we had. I went up to Broadcasting House. I went in and his show was an interactive show. He had Sian James on the phone from London. He asked me about the strike. I remember the first morning of the strike, my husband was on afternoons. I went off to work and passed the colliery on the way. I saw everyone had been picketed out. I rang him and said "Stay at home Stuart, you've been picketed out". But on the show someone had text in to say his uncle had 'scabbed' in the strike and he was still shunned in the pub 30 years later. He asked Sian and she dived in all political. So he asked me on air, I told Sian to shut up! 40 years before the strike the miners were the heroes of this country, we kept the wheels of industry going for us to win the war. 40 years later, those same men were trying to defend their jobs to feed their families, to pay their income tax, to pay their national insurance, and they were demonised. Some people will never understand there were people who tried to undermine us. I felt stitched up on the radio.

Not too long ago, I heard an interview with Bill Nighy. He obviously had no concept until he read the film script for Pride. He spoke so passionately about the struggles. I said to Stuart "Can you imagine that being on the radio 30 years ago?" We went from heroes to zeros and back to heroes again.

The things that stick in my mind about Hefina are that she was always well dressed. She was always warm, always hot! She had her tear duct that was blocked too and so she always had a tear rolling down her cheek. She had an amazing sense of humour and a larger than life personality. On a few occasions she would become very empathetic and supportive and that was a part of her too. She had a way of encouraging me without pushing me. She could see when I needed a push. I was always told to never use the word 'nice' when referring to a person, but Hefina was, she was a nice person. To be perfectly truthful, I would not have wanted to get on the wrong side of her! She was formidable! I felt safer with her than Edwina on the picket line. She was a steadying influence. She was clearly a very intelligent woman too. I think if she had been born in my generation then she would be off to university studying.

I can see her now, a smile on her face, the black dress with the frill around the neckline. She was the right person for each job she took on.

Everyone knew Hefina Headon. I don't ever remember her not being there! I admired her so much. I was aware of the problems she had in her younger life, we had some deep conversations throughout the years. She let go of a lot of little bits and I knew she'd had a rough time. I do think she was a very strong woman. I was very sad when I heard she had died.

What summed her up well was the words the minister read at her funeral, "She was born Hefina, she was known to friends, family and the community as Vina, but to her husband John, she was Hellfire!" I think Hellfire sums her up perfectly!

Friend

Mair Francis (Community Colleague & DOVE Workshop)

The first story I remember hearing about Hefina was when she used to allow the garden to be a short-cut, I thought that was wonderful, what a lovely lady to let people through. That told me a lot about Hefina.

I know she was active with so many organisations including the Pony Club, the Labour Party, the ATC, Seven Sisters CND and so many other groups.

I met Hefina through the Welsh school with the PTA (Parent Teacher Association). The first time was probably a committee meeting, about fundraising and I can imagine her there too. The Crynant mothers were quite active then. I was also the secretary of the CND back then with Doug Miller, Gwylym Morgan, Norman Burns and Joy Howells.

Hefina was so active in lots of little groups, when you wanted to have a committee, you would say Hefina would join, and so she did. Then the strike came in 1984. I thought she was a very jolly person and she was willing to take on anything. She was always reliable. She was highly regarded by everyone because everybody knew her.

I got more involved with Hefina with DOVE. She would come regularly to all the meetings. If we had a conference to go to, I would ask her and she would come. She loved those. She would know all the good chip shops along the way home! We used to use the red van that the LGSM gave us until it fell apart. The Open Cast mine gave us some money and we bought a new mini bus afterwards.

There was a film made when we went to Abernant to the picket line. Hefina and Edwina were picked up on the bus, Edwina was thumping a big drum and Hefina came dressed up, it may be 'Smiling and Splendid Women' made by the Swansea history group in the university. It was about women in the strike and about DOVE.

There was a great atmosphere up the DOVE, so much fun and lots of laughter, especially with Hefina and Edwina. Hefina was never confrontational, she was such an honest person, no snobbery or anything like that. DOVE grew from the grass roots. You would only provide something if you knew what the community needed. It was all about working locally with people. They knew what they wanted and we knew what they needed. We were lucky, it was the right time for the DOVE. I may get upset with some people but Hefina would be very supportive of me and everything that we wanted to do. She gave us 110%. Both her and Joy would say "Carry on doing the good work." Hefina was a real stalwart.

If you were setting up a campaign, you would know Hefina would come onside, especially if it had anything to do with the valley.

I regret not seeing her when she became ill. We were wrapped up in our own family life then. We did see her after she had a stroke, she wore a patch on her glasses. I believe she came up to DOVE, I think that was the last time I saw her.

Friend

Hywel Francis (Strike Committee Official & Former MP for Aberavon)

I first knew of Hefina when she worked at the Post Office in Onllwyn, I didn't know her to speak to, I just knew who she was. I knew she was involved in the Pony Club who would have met in the Onllwyn Welfare, I had other people who I knew that went there.

During the early days of the miners' strike, we saw that support groups were being set up mainly in Yorkshire. Some women had been to a big rally in Barnsley and they came back with a lot of enthusiasm, and it was partly to do with food distribution. I decided in conjunction with Phil Bowen, the former chair of the support group, to call a meeting and a large number of people turned up. Nobody knew how long the strike was going to last then.

The early meetings of the support group were held at the Double H (Miners' Welfare club) in Seven Sisters. I set up an account and I remained the treasurer. Hefina became the secretary and Phil Bowen was the chair. I then went to Russia and Christine became the treasurer while I was away. She was the natural person to take over as she was a teacher and a good friend of Hefina's. When we heard in late July that the funds were going to be sequestrated by the high court, we had to show there was a separation between the NUM and the support group so Phil Bowen stepped down and I became the chair.

We knew we had to do something as we realised people would be suffering some hardship. From the moment we set up the meeting, myself and Hefina became good friends. We had to trust one another. We had to do things that required a lot of personal trust.

Hefina was very central to it all. There were a number of women who were extremely strong. Hefina was one, Kay Bowen was another and Margaret Donovan another. They all had different roles. Hefina was at the centre, faithfully keeping the minutes and making sure decisions were being made. Kay really made sure that the food distribution worked like clockwork. Hefina didn't need to worry about that. We kept the men out of this part in order for it to run smoothly. In order to ensure the right things were done, the women had to have political power to do this which Kay made sure of. So in wielding the decisions in food distribution, that meant they had a lot of political power. Margaret Donovan led a completely separate part of the support group, identifying the need for a totally autonomous voice for women politically. They had their own aspirations and their own views about things, not just about the strike. She began to articulate that. She was the person who drove it. The men thought the women shouldn't do this, but they gave up fighting it.

There was a lot of activity in the months after the strike ended. Mair would drive the van donated by the LGSM. I would be on the loudspeaker with our son Sam. I also used to drive it. I would forget what was printed on the side, people would be looking at the sign and then looking at me. The sign said 'Lesbians and Gays Support the Miners'. Mair also had these experiences when she drove the van for the DOVE.

In the early days, it was Hefina who did most of the public speaking. She spoke in Seven Sisters and the following week in Pontyberem where she moved the resolution. She spoke in the big rally in the Avon Lido. I remember her telling me she had been asked to do this. She was seen as a leading figure across the whole coalfield. Right up until the moment we went into Cynheidre and when the gays arrived, it was Hefina, Kay and Margaret who were the key women. Edwina was also there but she was known as the 'troublemaker', if you wanted the big bass drum to make a big noise, she would be the one for that.

Hefina would be the person who went up to London from day 1 with Sian James. When we went to the Nottingham coalfield to provide support, Sian and Phil came then too. Hefina went to Durham and to the university in the September of 1984. She went up to North Wales as well. We still sustained the support group for some time afterwards. She went up for the Quarrymen's strike to support them too.

We had a number of women and men who were the backbone of the support group who were not directly involved with the pits, mostly widows and retired miners. That's what didn't exist in the other coalfields, we had generations of support. The extended family supported us too.

Hefina was important, she understood the need for a wider struggle. She had to take the arguments into the Labour Party. I noticed that she took it to the Seven Sisters ward. They summoned MP Donald Coleman to their meeting and she recorded this in the minutes. Wherever we were taking the struggle, she would be there.

Right at the very end there was a lot of upset and anger about the strike ending. The women picketed outside the Crynant welfare when Treforgan Colliery held a meeting to return to work.

We set up the Wales Congress and that was sustained. We re-launched it on 1st June, 1985 in Maesteg and Hefina was involved in that. Things came to an end with the support group in 1986.

In 1987 Hefina spoke at a fete at the DOVE Workshop. She continued to speak whenever she could. DOVE genuinely did move forward in a positive way and this created a natural continuity for Hefina. A lot of her energy was then channelled into DOVE and it remains one of the few good things that has come out of the strike. Of all the valleys in South Wales, the Dulais Valley has the few benign legacies of the strike, and they are all to do with women: DOVE, the women's rugby team in Seven Sisters along with the youth team and the new women's choir known as the Dulais Divas which Kay is now involved in.

In July 1997, the launch of the 'Yes for Wales' campaign was held in Cardiff Castle, Hefina came there with us. Hefina knew where the best chip shops were and we went to eat there.

We didn't see much of her once the years passed by, which we are sorry for.

Friend

David Donovan (Miners' Strike Committee Member)

I first met Hefina at one of our support group meetings on a Sunday. Hefina was our secretary and whilst I had not met her before she came across as very confident and able with a sense of humour.

My first impression was "Who is this woman that I have never seen before?" I say this because I believe that she was involved in the community before the strike and though we only lived a few miles apart and I was involved in the Labour Party in our valley, I had not met her before.

My first impressions didn't change. I came to respect her even more over time. Hefina showed herself to be a really nice woman, a combination of a woman who was experienced in committee work, very able, confident and had a sense of humour. I also felt that when she spoke she had the knowledge and strength to deliver because we were dealing with some very strong characters in the community and in the NUM (National Union of Mineworkers).

I felt that Hefina could be depended on. This is probably because I was very serious about the strike and the issues surrounding it. I believed that the NUM structure was incapable of sustaining the strike. Well, who could blame them, for this was a strike like no other. The strike needed to call on the families and the community which had not been necessary in the brief affairs of the 1970s and early 80s. So my serious outlook meant that I was drawn to people who were of a like mind who knew that everyone had to be called upon to support the NUM if the strike was to succeed.

I quickly began to realise that she was well known and liked in the community. She was very professional and able in a committee and knew how they worked. Once we left the meetings we knew Hefina would be working on things ready for the next time we met. She was meticulous with minutes, she always had a pad and a pen. She would write but always make eye contact too, showing an interest in the speaker and everyone in the room. She would turn to the person who spoke and would pay total attention to each person. Hefina was definitely a team player.

She was always properly dressed, never in tracksuits. She wasn't a very stiff person, she knew the courtesies when she needed them. This was a sign of her confidence. Inside her was that fighting spirit.

I had lost touch or rather I had not kept in touch with anyone from the strike once it had ended. I had not attended the anniversary events as I went to Ruskin College and got divorced from Margaret along the way. I was told by Stephen Beresford, the writer of the film, 'Pride', about Hefina's death, just after he had heard and I was really saddened. I was sad to hear of her dying but I understand now that she had not been well for some time. It seemed particularly sad as her actions in the strike were to be given such prominence by the making of 'Pride' and her character to be portrayed by a really important and fine actress. I have imagined Hefina being amused by the film being made and the recording of her actions. I imagine her looking at me the way she did when she was engaging with you and to be laughing at the prospect. I also think that she would be pleased inside for the recognition of the group she did so much to represent.

I only know about Hefina from those hectic months of the strike. However, my feelings towards her were full of respect because she had stepped up and played a role at a time when her community needed it. I was satisfied in my knowledge of Hefina which was that she delivered, and then some!

Friend

Sian James (Strike Activist & Beyond. Former MP for Swansea East)

I first met Hefina during the miners' strike of 1984. The women of the strike, from our faith, meant that we felt it was our role to come forward, to be active and to do something. It wasn't about advancement, not about putting yourself at the forefront, it was our duty to do it. We didn't force the way we felt, although we felt very strongly. I used to say "If Jesus was here, He would be on the picket lines with the miners." We were looking out for our communities, standing for everyone having a voice, standing for equality and standing for people treated badly.

I do wonder, if before the strike, I would have done the things I did if I had known what I know now. I judge everyone I meet now with one piece of criteria. Would I want that one person standing next to me on a picket line? Would I trust them? I know that Hefina and Edwina would have been either side of me. The commitment that was given by those strong women during this time was inspiring.

You were able to recognise kindred spirits as committed as you, people in other support groups, other women that you could trust. Hefina had made a journey like this years before the strike came around but for me this was the beginning. She was an exemplar.

I was asked in an interview once to describe Hefina. I had to say she wasn't like a mother to me, I had a mother and she had daughters of her own. I can't tell you what an impact she had on me. It was massive. Her and my mother were very different. Hefina taught me that there is no greater honour than serving your own community. It is satisfying, long reaching and life changing.

Hefina comes from a generation, like my mother, where when women became pregnant they finished work and the focus shifted to their children. Many jobs were not suitable for women who had children and were married. I remember the letter coming to the support group from the LGSM, a lot of people started to laugh, but very quickly it stopped. The women said if they collected the money then it's only courtesy to accept and send a letter of thanks. They soon came around. It was a brave new world, things had been challenged. It was time to hear from other people what the world was like.

The LGSM were a joy to be around. They were so safe and lovely. We were so comfortable to be with them and especially in London at that time. Hefina took it all in her stride, she always saw the best in people.

Hefina never expected anyone else to behave differently with her. I can't ever say that I saw Hefina intimidating anyone. She would wait to see what the reaction was and then move on from it. I used to encourage Margaret to stand up to Hefina, she would rather it this way and everyone would know where they stood and hopefully everyone was happy with the situation.

In the October of 1984, there was a public meeting in Neath town hall. Someone was speaking who wasn't very good, I turned to Hefina and told her I could do better with a paper bag on my head. She turned to Hywel Francis and told him "Sian wants to do public speaking!" so they put me down to do this. That Sunday night in the support group they were asked how everyone felt. This is where it started to show that the women were a good part of the support group. We weren't nagging our husbands to go back to work, instead we supported them to stay on strike. At the meeting, Hywel told Hefina and I that they wanted two speakers in London. We agreed to go together. Money for tickets was handed over to Hefina.

The next morning I went to Neath railway station. Myself and Hefina met up. When we got to Paddington, we had to make our way to Hackney. We had to ask the porter. We asked what tube to take. We thought the tube would take us everywhere! He told us to catch the buses. We weren't keen on this! Eventually we found the bus stop. Before we reached our stop the bus came to a halt. Everyone started to leave the bus, but we didn't, we sat at the back talking Welsh. We were very suspicious. A little old lady came over to us and told us we had to get off! We told her we weren't getting off! She said "You have to get off the bus, it has broken down!" We got to know each other very well after that trip.

Over time, the nation became more interested in how we were coping. The focus was shifting. We met a lot of people. We were spreading the word they wanted to hear. People had realised it was the women who were the big story of the strike which didn't sit too well with some of the men who felt threatened by this.

We had to go to Paddington one time in the car. There was a student demonstration going on and we would be supporting this. We would be marching past Westminster, then sitting down refusing to move from the bridge, so off we went! All the students were sat on the bridge and they wanted myself and Hefina to address them. They boosted us up onto the top of the bus stop and we addressed them from where we were, two sturdy women on a very sturdy bus stop! We had a very good relationship by this time.

We had our routine down to a tee by then. I would do the mother and about having children and then Hefina would talk about the community and after that we would collect the money that she would put into her trusty handbag.

At one of these events I had told Hefina I had never had a McDonalds, so she agreed that we could spend some of that day's lunch money on having a McDonalds. We had a burger and drank root beer! I enjoyed it but Hefina wasn't sure. She told me she couldn't taste or smell anything! These were the times we really got to know each other well.

We had a brilliant night one night, we were stood on a stage somewhere and I could feel someone behind me. I could feel their arms going up the back of my frock! I thought "What the hell?" It was Hefina. The buttons on my dress had come undone and she was doing them up for me, unobtrusively!

We were 90% solidly on strike. There was a meeting in Crynant, just before Christmas. We were all standing outside the Welfare Hall. We were really angry as the men were talking about going back. We were saying "Don't forget the sacked and jailed men." Hefina was there. Imogen, our friend and supporter, took a photo where Hefina was stood in a rain coat with her hat, high heels and her handbag!

Rowena, my daughter, used to ask Hefina in Welsh, "How can you walk in those heels?" She would wear her stilettos everywhere! The miners began to slowly trickle back to work after this meeting.

We had money from the support group to go on trips. We went to Caswell Bay once. Off Edwina and Hefina went. When they returned there was a stir. Everyone started to laugh. Down they came in a full Victorian bathing costume, with two big black hand marks on her boobs and two on her bum, and a big sign on her back stating 'I'm married to a miner'. The whole beach was rolling around!

One time, the women were accused of having secret meetings. We were called up in front of the NUM. We were carpeted, standing in front of the executive and asked why we were supporting Arthur Scargill. By this point we had gone off on a tangent. We didn't understand why after fighting for over a year it all collapsed and a phased return to work was implemented.

When the news had come through that Hefina's daughter, Jennifer had died, I remember going over to see her. John opened the door. He told me "She's been waiting for you to come." We had been a bit late. He was a bit cross, which was strange for John and his laid back personality. Hefina knew that I could understand what she was feeling and the effect something like this can have on someone. I remember there being an offer to bring her body back, but Hefina declined. She knew Jennifer loved America and so she should stay. This made the grieving process more prolonged.

We would have conversations like "Jayne's going to be one of Maggie's boot girls!" I would tell Hefina not to say things like that as Jayne wasn't like that, but she wouldn't listen. This was her way of dealing with another child leaving home. She had to make a big thing of it. When Jayne wrote about the explosion that happened in Germany in the barracks from the IRA attack on the Sergeant's Mess in 1987, where the windows had blown in and and everyone was in a panic. We were all a mess. If Hefina could have got on a plane then she would have gone over and rescued her! These times gave her an opportunity to talk about her feelings to me.

Hefina was so proud of her grandchildren. I didn't know anyone who could be so proud. She really respected what her children had all done. She was a very stoic woman, in the sense of what couldn't be cured had to be endured. We dealt with it, we made it better, we found a way.

Hefina had a wicked sense of humour, she was a cheeky one! A particular memory I have is of John and Hefina dancing, they were so light on their feet. I can see them now, pure elegance. The first time I saw them dancing like that I thought "Bloody hell, they are good!" They were very alive. She always had a lovely bearing, always glamorous. This is where I saw the similarities of her and my mother. With Hefina, everything had to be right.

The hair lacquer she used to make herself at home, and the dispenser she would use would make the air thick. We needed gas masks. I remember not having any once and I borrowed hers. It was so sticky in my hands and my hair was stiff as a board!

Hefina was such an inspiration, she definitely was for me. I have such happy memories of her.

Friend

Mike Jackson – (Member of LGSM ⟋ Lesbians & Gays Support the Miners)

My first encounter of Hefina was when I wrote to her before I met her. It was the letter of introduction between LGSM and Dulais. I met her on the Saturday of our first visit to Wales.

On first meeting Hefina, she instantly reminded me of my Grandma, who I adored. Grandma died two years previously, in 1982. They were of a similar build and height. They were both strong matriarchs who knew how to deal with their menfolk, husbands, brothers, sons, friends. They were both working class women and had evolved in industrial working class communities where the men had brutal jobs. Brutal jobs can lead to brutalisation but these women understood this and were determined to bring up their families decently. They made sure that their menfolk were accountable to their families and if needs be they would assert boundaries of acceptable and unacceptable behaviour. In my experience, the menfolk always gave way to women like this, maybe a little protest here and there but in the end they stood by their womenfolk. So for me, it was an instant recognition of who Hefina was and an instant love for her.

Our relationship started off so well and over time it just deepened. She just re-affirmed all those positive regards I had for women from working class backgrounds who were intelligent, firm, compassionate, fun and strong.

We had a special relationship because we were counterparts, we were both secretaries of our miners' support groups and corresponded by letter and phone calls. The very first visit in October, 1984 we all got on a coach to go to a rally in Swansea. Hefina was walking up and down the coach introducing herself and trying to make everyone feel comfortable. One of our gang was a woman who had no experience of working class life and told Hefina that she didn't really drink (alcohol). Given that there was going to be a social at the Onllwyn later that night, Hefina said Loudly "X tells me that she doesn't drink! Well we'll have to do something about that when we get back!" The woman blanched and I giggled. She was such a stuck up person anyway.

I last saw her a year or two later (maybe longer) at a reunion in Wales.

We went back to someone's house, probably after the Onllwyn. I think that John had died by then. She was still holding court and I remember thinking how she was so revered by the entire community

I have recently seen a lovely, funny photo of her carrying John in her arms and both of them laughing.

I was prepared to hear that she, one day would have passed away. Jayne had forwarded me that Hefina was ill and so I was somewhat expecting the news.

Hefina was a hero but like most working class people, particularly the women, she would have passed away without any long-term history of her achievements except for the memories of her immediate family and friends. I'm so pleased that her memory is there in perpetuity because of Pride the movie.

Friends

Reggie Blennerhassett & Ray Alner (Members of LGSM)

This was a joint discussion:

Reggie: I first met Hefina when I came down to Wales for the first time. I think it was in October, 1984 the first trip. There were 26 of us in three vans. We were late because we got lost. On the next night we came to the Welfare Hall and met Hefina, I remember her as being so welcoming. When we walked in everyone was welcoming but Hefina in particular. You got the impression straight away that she wasn't one to be messed with. She seemed to have a huge amount of respect from the people she worked with.

We came into contact with Hefina on a number of occasions in Wales and in London when she came with the group. We were involved in organising the Pits and Perverts concert in the Electric Ballroom in Camden. There was a group that came and we met them. We took them out in London. She had a sense of fun.

On one occasion the van came to London. I remember being in the van driving around London, and people would double take, they couldn't believe what they were seeing from the signage on the van that read 'Lesbians and Gay Men Support the Miners'.

I also remember the trip when we all went on the river. That was another fantastic trip.

Ray: I wasn't on the first trip, I came on the second trip down, and as Reggie says, the energy was buzzing off Hefina. She was such a fun character. She always seemed very grounded. She had a great force of personality and charisma, you could see that she was in charge. Again when she came up to London, I saw a great sense of fun indeed.

Reggie: I remember one time when we were dancing in a group at the Onllwyn Welfare hall and a group of local lads came in. Some of them came over to us and started pushing us slightly when we were dancing. Hefina and all the women formed a circle around us and basically got rid of the lads from around us. It was incredible, that was the only time anything like that actually happened.

Ray: Yes she told them to leave us alone.

Reggie: Another occasion I do remember was the Whitehall march. Hefina was on that march too, everyone came on the march with us. It was a march through London and it was a big family event; there were children there too. Again there was a great sense of fun and a sense of passion about what we were protesting against, but then it turned very ugly, they forced everyone into a space which was a frightening event.

Ray: I remember that day, I know Hefina turned and faced the police, she was shouting at them. It was frightening, they would charge us with horses if they needed to.

Reggie: She always spoke well and very passionately; she was great to listen to. Nothing seemed to faze her.

Ray: I feel she was a beacon for the other women, helping them to believe that they too could do these things. Her enthusiasm was a big enabling force.

Reggie: We weren't aware if there was any resistance between the support we gave from LGSM within the community because we didn't hear about this if there was any. The film. 'Pride' portrays this but I don't believe it was actually there.

Ray: Sian told us that there wasn't really much resistance, maybe a few seconds we weren't taken seriously but then that went and they accepted us and the money we raised.

Reggie: I am always interested to know about the van, we didn't expect anything from it, we just gave the money and that was it. It would have been interesting to know what people were saying during the decision to put the sign on the doors of the van for LGSM. It was such a big statement to make.

I have another story but I am not sure if it was Hefina who told us, it's about the food coming in from Italy. Loads of pasta arrived and they didn't know what to do with it. They thought it was breakfast cereal! I think some of the food that came in was a bit obscure.

I used to remember sitting at the tables in the Onllwyn Welfare and playing bingo. These nights were such great fun, we really enjoyed our visits there.

It was great to have Stephen Beresford, the writer of the film, 'Pride', stand in our home and tell us the story of the film. After the film we have had a lot of people come up to us and tell us they had no idea about the story. There has been such a fantastic response.

Friend

Roy James – (Member of LGSM)

I remember Sian staying at my flat in Hackney on a number of occasions and Hefina came over as we were all meeting up before going out on the town. I often wondered what they told the men back home about what went on when the girls came up to London. Our flat was equi-distant between the LA and the Fallen Angel (bars in London).

There was a lot of money being spent on the bars in the mid-eighties, so they were glamorous and less 'dark' than the film portrays. There were bars like First Out at Tottenham Court Road and the Fallen Angel in Islington that were 'Euro Cafes', which were all-comers welcome, so was the Bell, of course.

It must have been fascinating to the miners' support group in Wales (Neath, Dulais and Swansea Valleys Miners' Support Group) to meet the mixed group of people that formed LGSM. This was clear every time we met Hefina, Sian, Margaret and Yvonne when they came to London. There was a genuine search for knowledge and understanding about our lives as gay men. This sharing of knowledge about our respective communities formed the underlying bond that continued after the strike was over. We were all conscious that this bond was formed by the oppression that both groups felt from the Thatcher government at the time.

LGSM consisted of around 30-50 gay men in the main, apart from Stephanie, who was a close friend of Reggie and Ray. The majority of those gay men would have considered themselves to be gay activists but were unaligned to any political party or communist/Trotskyist cult, albeit that they would have considered themselves to be on the far left as a result of their sexual politics. Most, if not all, would have been 'pluralist' in their politics, i.e. anti-sexist and anti-racist and 'anti' any other form of discrimination.

Many of the gay men in LGSM were from working class origins outside of London but had moved to London both to get work and to live their lives as gay men. I moved to London in 1973, which was when gay liberation was being established in the UK after its emergence after Stonewall in the USA. My involvement with LGSM was due to my having come from a mining background in the Midlands. Many of my relatives worked either in the mines or in the steel factories. My first proper job after leaving school was as a trainee estates surveyor for the National Coal Board (NCB) at Markham Colliery in North-East Derbyshire. I was 19 years old at the time. I joined LGSM because I was appalled that the proposed pit closures under Thatcher would rip the economic heart out of working class communities that were often dependent on only one industry such as mining.

There was an immediate complementary fascination between the LGSM gay men and the small group of miners' wives led by Hefina. The others always asked Hefina for her views whenever a difficult topic was being discussed. It was not long before we discovered that these women had aligned not only through their child-care, but also through their respective Christian faiths, CND, Greenham Common, and the Labour Party, which no doubt led to them joining the Neath, Dulais and Swansea Valley Miners' Support Group. On a less serious note we, in LGSM, really enjoyed taking our Welsh visitors to various gay pubs and clubs that were welcoming to all. This was not difficult as there was a shift in the 1980s to gay pubs and clubs that had more open-door policies as part of their strategy to be more visible in the community, not least by not blacking-out the windows and by having open outside areas that were a source of interest to passers-by.

There was an unsurprising division around age in LGSM. Put crudely, the two age groups comprised being either under or over twenty five years old. This was in addition to the range of political divisions within LGSM, which was broadly around whether the grouping was Stalinist or more libertarian in their communist or socialist views. The division around age was very significant as HIV and AIDS was then seen as being exclusively the problem of older gay men. It should be noted that being older in LGSM was being around thirty years old but this had its advantages to some extent, as it meant that we were around the same age as our Welsh counterparts.

It was in common circulation at the time that the groups of gay men at higher risk of infection and, therefore, to be avoided, were Americans, Haitians, older gay men and 'clones' (gay men who wore moustaches, checked shirts, and '501's). The latter were portrayed by many on the gay left as being capitalistic so were vilified. My view at the time was that this simplistic view of 'clones' was a smoke screen for the reactionary fears about HIV and AIDS held by many who purported to be radical gay men. It is not without it's note that Mark Ashton, along with so many of us, changed his appearance at the time from that of a clone to being more outré, that of a dandy.

The ambivalence towards and maltreatment of those older gay men was moderated as the group developed, due in large part to the influence of people like Hefina. There was a centrality to the group in Wales, which was that of the Labour Party, and which stood in sharp contrast to the wide range of political divisions within LGSM. Being a communist would not have been unusual to the Welsh community given the popularity of the Communist Party of Great Britain in mining communities. Ironically the shock-value of being on the ultra-left was lost on the Welsh. However, it is worth noting that the communism in mining communities was not Marxist in origin. There is a phrase in British socialism, which is that 'British Socialism has more to do with Methodism (i.e. the chapel and Christianity) than Marxism'. This form of communism was based in egalitarianism, i.e. everyone should be treated equally regardless of their background.

This egalitarian political position was clearly Hefina's own position, and that of the other women in Wales. Hefina was the most confident of those women and self-assured in her view that no-one should be ostracised for the dreadful health issue that was, and still is, HIV and AIDS. This support had a huge impact on the gay men within LGSM. We were completely accepted and celebrated and this was at a time when HIV/AIDS was generally misunderstood as a social phenomenon with a lot of misinformation as a result. No one at the time had any real view of how to deal with this issue socially let alone medically. For us to be accepted and cared for by these amazing women when no one had any real idea of the consequences was totally humbling.

Ironically, we were all put under heavy manners by some of the Welsh women, when we were in the presence of Hefina with regards to Cliff. We were under strict instructions not to mention his sexual preferences to Hefina. This was unproblematic, as it would not have been appropriate to do so if Cliff had chosen not to have that discussion with Hefina. It was not for us to 'out' him particularly, as it seemed likely that Hefina might well have decided to avoid raising the issue in order to protect Cliff from having to be an 'out' gay man in his own community. I had a good deal of sympathy with this position having chosen to leave my own community and move south to London for those very reasons.

Friends

Elizabeth & Kirby Porter (Strike Supporters)

As told by Elizabeth

We first met Hefina when she was brought to our home in Leyton, London, by Dai Donovan. Sian James was with her. They had come up to London during the miners' strike to speak at a meeting. I wasn't expecting them and Dai just knew he could bring them for their dinner. I remember it was a Thursday night. Kirby, my husband was working late in Haringey Libraries. I always did my supermarket shopping on Friday so there wasn't much in the house for unexpected guests but I managed to make them a two-course meal. I don't remember the main course but I do remember the dessert. It was apples with a crumble topping, to which I had added some Original Crunchy cereal to make it a bit more interesting. Anyway they enjoyed it and we had a good time.

My first impression was of a very strong and determined woman who wanted to get the best for her community, whatever it took. She was a real fighter! This didn't change over time. The next time we saw her was in Wales, at the Sunday meeting of the miners' support group. We saw how well respected she was by everyone in it. We were impressed with her contribution at the meeting. We saw how extraordinary ordinary people could be if they were fighting for something they believed in.

Hefina never forgot the people who had supported her and her community and kept in touch with us via Christmas cards and letters until she died. She also wrote to me to say she was visiting her daughter Jayne in Lisburn army camp and she would like to visit us. It was lovely to see her again but she had aged quite a lot by then and wasn't so lively. We were regretting moving from London and less lively ourselves and there was no good news from the mining communities at that time.

When we heard she had passed away we were very sad but felt she had made the absolute most of her life and that that was a great thing. We knew she would be much missed.

I think her life is a testament to what women in every community can achieve when circumstances dictate that to survive they need to fight in an extraordinary way to make things better for their families and their communities. I thought it was great that she wasn't intimidated by the fact that the whole weight of the state was ranged against the miners. She was determined to make head way!

We recently visited South Wales again for the 30th Anniversary night in the Onllwyn Welfare Hall. That was the first time we had been back since shortly after the strike. We were apprehensive that, with all the pits closed, the community would have been destroyed, but it was the complete opposite of that. We found that the community was still strong and ready to fight for what they believed in. The fact that the community survived and wasn't destroyed by Thatcher is a testament to the work of Hefina and others like her! I came away uplifted and encouraged with hope for the future. It was very obvious from everyone there how respected her memory still is.

And so we have come to the end.

Fair play to you all.

"You Said It!"

Acknowledgements

Firstly I would like to thank my late mother, Hefina, for being such an outstanding woman, who has inspired and driven me to writing her life story, spurning me on to collect as much information as I could about this formidable woman.

I would especially like to thank my partner Emily, who has endured days and evenings of being ignored, for reading my every written word and correcting my grammar and spelling. Without her I would not have made it past the first draft.

I want to thank my brother Ian Headon and my sister Alison Williams for the bombardment of random text messages asking all sorts of strange questions, and spending time going over their own memories to piece events together.

I also thank my sons Sean, Owen and Gregg who have listened to me tell them story after story about family they didn't know they had, showing them photographs of the past and repeating myself endlessly about my chapters and my jaunts.

A very big thank you also goes to all of the family who have been nagged to send me information, spending time sharing their memories, Alex and Daniel Williams, Christopher, Mathew and Ashley Headon, little Ffion Haf Williams, my sister in law Jackie Headon and my brother in law Russell Williams and my ex husband Stuart Meldrum.

Thank you too for the memories given by my Auntie Mary (Lewis) and Uncle Dennis (Newton), who are the last two remaining of Hefina's generation. Thank you too for the time I spent with all my cousins; Christine Woozley, Monica Thomas, Erica Jones, Andrea Newton Mills, Helen Bankhead, Kath Bamford Mason, Martyn Bamford, Sara McNamara, Janice Hacker West, Terrill Phillips, Christine Scarratt, and Janice Lavercombe.

It was challenging contacting those who were willing and available to help me. For their time and digging deep into their memories, I would like to thank all those who touched Hefina's life in one way or another and who have shared this with me.

Betsy Becker, Carole Westall MBE, Christine Powell, Derek Tong,

Joy Howells, Sian James, Hywel and Mair Francis, David Donovan, Valerie James, Ann and Malcolm Hathaway, Janice Jones, Peter Lloyd, Emyr Lewis, Iris Bevan, Reggie Blennerhassett, Ray Aller, Mike Jackson, Rhian Loosemore, Roy James, Dennis Whitney and Elizabeth and Kirby Porter.

Once the film Pride came to fruition, Sophie Glover of Pathé received endless emails from me, I thank her and the Pathé team for allowing me to use the production notes from the film.

Thank you to all who provided me with permission to reproduce and publish their images and articles: Nicholas Parry of the South Wales Eveing Post, Tony Woolway of Media Wales, Louise Carolin of DIVA Magazine and Kevin Franklin. The staff at the Richard Burton Archive at Swansea University were very accommodating when we visited to research the minutes of the miners' support group meeting and put up with our chatting, thank you.

To my cousin Andrea Newton Mills for reading through the final manuscript. Thank you for the advice given to me by Gemma Coles on how to become a self publisher and putting me in touch with Dyrck Lamble of Caktus Printing who has given us this book in its physical form.

Finally a big thank you to my review team who have provided me with an insight into what people might think of this book. Val Smith, Jeanette Findon, Cleo Thompson, Gill Davies, Nicola Scott, Linda Hatton and Laura Collins.

'Diolch yn fawr i chi gyd'.

A guide to Welsh pronounciation

THE WELSH ALPHABET: (28 letters)

A, B ,C ,Ch, D, Dd, E, F, Ff, G, Ng, H, I, L

Ll, M, N, O, P, Ph, R, Rh, S, T, Th, U, W, Y

(Note that Welsh does not possess the letters J, K, Q, V, X or Z, though you will often come across "borrowings" from English, such as John, Jones, Jam and Jiwbil (Jubilee); Wrexham (Wrecsam); Zw (Zoo).

THE VOWELS: (A, E, I, U, O, W, Y)

A as in man. Welsh words: am, ac Pronounced the same as in English)

E as in bet or echo.

I as in pin or queen.

U as in pure.

O as in lot or moe.

W as in Zoo or bus.

Y has two distinct sounds: the final sound in happy or the vowel sound in myrrh.

THE DIPHTHONGS:

Ae, Ai and Au are pronounced as English "eye"

Eu and Ei are pronounced the same way as the English ay in pray.

Ew is more difficult to describe. It can be approximated as eh-oo or perhaps as in the word mount. The nearest English sound is found in English midland dialect words such as the Birmingham pronunciation of "you" (yew).

I'w and Y'w sound almost identical to the English "Ee-you." or "Yew" or "You"

Oe is similar to the English Oy or Oi.

Ow is pronounced as in the English tow, or low.

Wy as in English wi in win or oo-ee.

Ywy is pronounced as in English Howie.

Aw as in the English cow.

THE CONSONANTS:

For the most part b, d, h, l, m, n, p, r, s, and t are pronounced the same as their English equivalents (h is always pronounced, never silent). Those that differ are as follows:

C always as in cat; never as in since.

Ch as in the Scottish loch or the German ach or noch. The sound is never as in church, but as in loch or Docherty.

Dd is pronounced like the English th in the words seethe or them.

Th is like the English th in words such as think, forth, thank.

F as in the English V.

Ff as in the English f.

G always as in English goat, gore.

Ng as in English finger or Long Island. Ng usually occurs with an h following as a mutation of c.

Ll is an aspirated L. That means you form your lips and tongue to pronounce L, but then you blow air gently around the sides of the tongue instead of saying anything. Got it? The nearest you can get to this sound in English is to pronounce it as an l with a th in front of it.

Rh sounds as if the h come before the r. There is a slight blowing out of air before the r is pronounces.   Brittania Online

TRANSLATIONS WITHIN THE BOOK

Mehefin	June
Mynydd	Mountain
Mŵg	Smoke
Ty Back	Little house (toilet)
Annibynnol	An independent Christian faith
Eglwys	Chapel
Mamgu	Grandmother
Dadcu	Grandfather
Hen Mamgu	Old grandmother
Fawr	Big
Fach	Small
Cwm	Valley
Dere 'ma	Come here
Gymanfa Ganu	Singing Festival
Cawl Cennin	Welsh Leek and potato soup
Twmpath Dawns	Welsh Folk Dancing
Cawl	Stew
Ysgol	School
Gynradd	Primary
Gyfyn	Comprehensive
Gymraeg	Welsh

Reference and Bibliography

Books:

Francis, M. (2008) *Up The Dove, The History of the DOVE Workshop in Banwen.* View (DOVE) Banwen.

Francis. H, (2015) *History on our side, Wales and the 1984-85 Miners' Stirke.* Lawrence & Wishart. London

Lewis, T.I. (2005) *The Brief History of Blaendulais Seven Sisters.* Andreas Haaf & Son. Port Talbot. [Taken from the original self written documents of 1966]

Lewis, T.I. (2003) *The Ideal Miner.* Lifestory publishing. Neath.

Young, I et. al. (1986) *Striking Women, Communities & Coal.* Pluto Press. London.

Journals & Meeting Notes:

Francis. M, (1995) *Women and the Aftermath of the strike 1984-85 Miners' Strike, A South Wales analysis.* Degree of MSc Thesis, University of Wales, Swansea.

Headon, H. (1984-85) *Meeting Minutes.* Onllwyn. Neath, Dulais & Swansea Valley Miners' Support Group.

James. V, (2010) The Melin Family Photobook. Online publisher

Online:

No Author (2015) Celtic Welsh Language [online] [July 2015] Available from: http://www.britannia.com/celtic/wales/language.html

No Author (2015) Childhood cancer awareness [online] [October 2014] Available from: http://leukaemialymphomaresearch.org.uk/childhood-cancer-awareness-month/milestones-treatment-childhood-leukaemia/1960s

No Author (n.d.) Cwm Dulais Historical Society [online] [October 2014] Available from: http://cwmdulais.org

No Author (2015) DOVE Workshop [online] [November 2014] Available from: http://www.doveworkshop.org.uk/about-us/

No Author (2015) History of the bombing of Swansea Docks [online] [September 2014] Available at www.explore-gower.co.uk/explore/swansea/world-war-two/

No Author (n.d.) South Wales Miners Strike [online] [December 2014] Available from: http://www.walesonline.co.uk/news/local-news/